The Way of the Initiate

By Roy Eugene Davis

CSA Press
Lakemont, Georgia 30552
1970

Copyright 1968
by Roy Eugene Davis

Standard Book Number 87707-012-1

Printed in the United States of America

CONTENTS

Introduction 5

CHAPTER ONE
The Totality of Being 25

CHAPTER TWO
Genesis Unveiled 35

CHAPTER THREE
Ten Thousand Years of Light 55

CHAPTER FOUR
The Lightbearers 65

CHAPTER FIVE
The Glorious Destiny 77

CHAPTER SIX
Steps to Mystical Experience 89

CHAPTER SEVEN
Seven Levels of Soul Unfoldment 99

CHAPTER EIGHT
Exploring the Inner Worlds 113

CHAPTER NINE
The Revelation of the Supreme Self 127

CHAPTER TEN
The Final Perfection 137

INTRODUCTION

The Eternal Religion

Introduction

The Way of An Initiate is not an esoteric work designed for a special few, but a guide for all who would walk the path which leads to complete Self-realization. In this book you will find yourself. *You will learn where you came from, what you are to do in this world and ultimately how to arrive at the realization of the Absolute Self.* Here you will find the essential principles which are not contingent upon ill-founded facts, unscientific beliefs or arbitrary imaginative visions. May it give utterance to the aspirations of all men and women who seek the Light.

This material is not new for there are no unique revelations. What is recorded is merely the restatement of eternal truths in the language of our time, without compromise and without any attempt to popularize the message. The truths of spirit can be intuitively comprehended only by those who prepare themselves by clearing the mind and consciousness. We *must* purge the mind of all distraction and cleanse the consciousness from all darkness to acquire spiritual wisdom. The clear perception of truth results in the renewal of life. The realm of spirit is not separate from the realm of manifest life of creation. There is no division in truth. In these pages you will learn to rise above the dualities and view the cosmic panorama as it is. The true illumined soul acts as a member of the kingdom of God, *transforming the world and becoming a savior to others.* It is possible to live in this world and still remain aware of the Highest Self, the transcendental aspect of spirit.

I have attempted to impart a vision of truth both impressive and profound and to open up new pathways for the mind of man. Here is a comprehensive synthesis of vital elements, a refinement and reconciliation of different currents of thought and feeling. After all, all genuine spiritual movements and true divine feelings at last converge towards the same end—the liberation of man. You will also find a number of different suggestions about the nature of the Absolute and Its relation to creation. You may even find this book to be the key which opens the mystery to the scriptures of the world.

When we study the words of truth reverently, we receive as much living spiritual influence as we are capable of accepting. Reality is *that which Is*. It is beyond conditioning and human comprehension. The entire world with its various manifestations is but a reflection of the formless Reality which exists in Its transcendental aloneness. A soul which is deluded finds its vision to be obscured; thus it is ensnared in the cosmic process, the endless chain of causes and effects. Only when the soul awakens to realize that its nature is the same as the Universal Reality can it be free. When this happens the ego is dissolved, the sense of separateness is removed, the wandering ceases and the soul rests in blissful self-recognition.

No action or religious ritual can redeem man because *liberation is due to awakening and is not the effect of of any human cause*. Any action performed to cause a reaction is an indication of spiritual blindness and has to do only with this relative world.

Pure Spirit is without attributes and cannot be understood by a mind which is accustomed to using concepts or pictures. Only when the soul nature is awakened so that the intuition is active can the true nature of Spirit be known. God is unrecognized until one is born again, awakened to a larger dimension of reality. Outwardly, a deluded person may not appear to be different from an illumined one; but *inwardly* there is no self-delusion. There is the clear perception of truth. The illumined soul knows itself to be an individualization of Spirit, as the wave is but an appearance on the surface of the ocean and has its real being and power in the larger body. The illumined soul is God in action. There is nothing we can do to become spiritual. We can, however, attempt to clear the mind and consciousness so that the light of the soul can shine of its own accord. We are not creating a free condition. We are *awakening to the realization of that which has always been true of ourselves.*

The sages, at different times and in different places have prescribed various ways to liberation. We will consider many of these ways in the pages which follow and pay attention to the essential suggestions and practical methods. Only spiritual experience can provide us with proofs of the existence of Spirit. The mystery of Reality is not to be solved by intellectual exercise for the true vision is a *beyond-the-mind* perception. Spirit is identical with the deepest self of man for it is Spirit which is *individualized* as the soul.

We cannot describe pure Being. All of our descriptions, as seemingly lucid as they may be, are halting and imperfect. We cannot even name It although many have tried to do so. True attainment of the cosmic vision implies non-discussion although one who is resting at the edge of cosmic vision tends to have compassion upon all who do not even suspect its existence and upon those who inwardly feel its existence but do not know how to perceive it. Jesus, Buddha and other enlightened ones maintained silence when questioned about the nature of the Supreme Reality because no words can describe it to one in whom intuition is not aroused. Yet, out of this indescribable Being has come all outward manifestation. It has appeared as that which is perceived as well as That which perceives. *The Eternal Reality not only supports existence but is the active power in the world and appears as all things.*

The world is meaningful and has purpose. True mystics have always attempted to maintain the stability of the social order and to cooperate in keeping the movement of the things of nature in balance. Because Reality is in one aspect, formless and transcendental, we are not to disregard our responsibilities in the world as long as the world has use or a reason for being. While it may not be immediately possible to understand the reason for creation, the fact that creation exists is an indication that there is purpose for it. It is the nature of life to express in various ways.

There are two ways of looking at the Eternal. The Supreme Reality, in its absolute self-existence is Spirit, pure and unconditioned. However, as the creative and controlling aspect It is God. Considering things from this point of view one might conclude that there is a Reality beyond God, a consideration which even reasonable men try to avoid even though That which is beyond God must be the cause and sustainer of God. The Supreme Self is, at the same time; the transcendental, the cosmic and the individual reality. *Pure being, God and the soul are different degrees of the same thing.*

God, the controlling aspect of Spirit, is also the cause of darkness or what men term *evil. It is all relative* when we see it from the correct point of view. When we are involved in darkness and confusion the negative aspect is hard to understand, yet it is but part of a beautiful and orderly plan when surveyed from the vantage point of cosmic consciousness. In the world we can easily see that there is a struggle between opposing forces. There are positive and negative tendencies which lead either to enlightenment or further into bondage according to whether or not we are successful in our ability to know the Truth. God is omnipotent because, being All, there are no external limits to His power. God, the controlling aspect of pure Being certainly knows all. Seeing the tendencies, God sees also the results for man. God is playing all the roles. A person who fears God or who refuses to try to understand the nature of God or who denies the existence of God merely does not know the true nature of God. To repeat, *God is the outer controlling aspect of pure Being.* In God there is no condemnation, no urge to punish or reward. God merely keeps the play going until souls are redeemed or until the worlds are dissolved. Nature is law abiding. There is order and an inexhaustible motive power in the universe. While deluded souls may seem to have a will of their own as they wander in darkness, they cannot avoid their ultimate fate: to awaken and know themselves as God. It matters not whether the realization comes in years or centuries, it will certainly come. This is sure. After all, Spirit has individualized as the soul. Can Spirit lose Itself? Can Spirit forget Itself? Of course it is impossible for the soul not to awaken and know the truth about itself.

God, the outward manifestation of Spirit, is responsible for the creation, preservation and dissolution of the universe. The Supreme has two sides to its nature, the higher and the lower. The higher represents the souls and the lower represents the material medium, the stuff of the world, the substance of creation. It is, therefore, the soul or life essence and also; the body, as well as the world. Just as the worlds were sent forth into manifestation, so they are sustained and will eventually be purified and dissolved.

It is hard for the average person to understand why creation has come into manifestation at all if it is to eventually be dissolved. No amount of philosophical speculation can explain it because the mind is limited by inadequate information. One might despair at the impossibility of it all if it were not for the realization, even though dim, that at the core of our being we *already know* the answers to the most impossible questions.

In the world we become aware of a seeming duality. We know that Spirit is beyond creation, even though It is the cause and sustainer of it. The Absolute is impersonal and untouched by anything that happens in creation. Yet, It controls and regulates all happenings. All shadings, colorings, forms, concepts, ideas of time and space, motion and particles of matter exist in Spirit. The world in which we live is actual, it exists, *but it is not as it appears to us as we perceive it through the senses.*

No matter how difficult life seems to be, we are, according to the enlightened teachers, to take refuge in Spirit. At the final hour we can be transformed if we will but remember three things. "I am indestructible, I am changeless and immovable, I am the essence of Life." Even the incarnations of God cannot save us though they may stand as examples and impart their wisdom. Only our own awakened consciousness can save us from self-delusion and its consequent suffering. Self-abandonment results in transfiguration. Our goal on earth is to manifest pure Spirit. The indwelling Spirit is to, in time, come forth and be revealed in each one of us. Spirit exists in and as millions of forms on earth. Through some forms the light shines brightly and we behold pure Light and Life. Through the masses the light scarcely glimmers at all. Illumined souls are few in contrast with the many incarnated beings but they demonstrate what all must realize.

God is not only in all creatures but is the *essence, life and reality of all.* God even expresses as the one which suffers. Universal suffering is the result of mass ignorance, lack of spiritual understanding. Animals and men suffer pain, failure, frustration and seeming death. This is all due to the fact that souls are sleeping in relationship to their true nature. They sleep and they dream the mortal dream. But, all souls will one day awaken and the dreams will fade away for they are but *fabrications of the deluded mind*, the medium which forms all manifestations.

In the most pressing of times, the activity of God is present. From the blackest of nights the glorious radiance can shine, revealing the mysteries and revelations of Spirit. When our glorified human nature is purified, when our understanding is cleansed, the light of pure consciousness is reflected in it. Often, when all seems lost, the inner light flashes forth and all is made new, bright and worthwhile. Then does man receive the Divine light, hear the Divine voice and act in Divine power. Then is the embodied consciousness revealed to be the *unborn eternal*.

Unawakened man struggles with the forces of nature, falsehood, limitation and a sense of mortality. His whole being is bewildered and there seems to be no way out. Then, if he is wise, he turns to his higher self, to Spirit, and appeals for grace and true enlightenment. His sincere desire leads him to a teacher who embodies the truth or to a clear teaching which has been prepared by one who is wise in the knowledge of spiritual things. He begins to walk the spiritual path which leads to perfect realization and complete freedom.

There is conflict in the minds of many earnest seekers as to the true nature of the world. Is it real? Does it exist? What is it and how does it exist? These are questions which haunt the quiet hours. Creation is not an illusion. *It is a projection from the mind of God, an externalization of pictures contained in the universal mind*, of which more will be learned in succeeding chapters.

Every religion teaches that the Supreme Reality is beyond time and space. God dwells, we are told, in the ever-existent-now, seeing the beginning, the end and all that goes on between. The truth is that God is both beyond the time order and is also fully involved with every minute process in creation. Not a sparrow falls, not a blade of grass wilts, not a creature is born, except God knows. Is this incomprehensible? Then let it be for a time.

Formless Spirit and manifest creation are two poles of the one Reality. We are not to think in terms of God and creation, but of God *as* creation. Yet, manifest creation is subordinate to the transcendental aspect of Reality. The entire cosmic process is the interaction between the two principles of being and non-being. The upper limit is God and the lower is nature. The cosmic process is Spirit working through and as nature, which seems to have the power of resistance because Spirit imparted it with a tenacious urgency to persist. This resistance of nature to the molding action of Spirit gives rise to what men call evil, though evil has no existence of its own. It is not another power. While it may seemingly resist, because the play must go on, there is never a possibility of its overcoming Spirit, for Spirit is the cause of it, as with everything else.

Creation is necessary for the drama of life. The world is what it is because of tension and the tension is the result of dual forces, both emanating from God, the Supreme Reality. When the universe gives in to the attracting pull of Spirit, it will be delivered from bondage and completely illuminated. *The worlds will cease to be and all will be restored to original pure Being.*

Why is there the precipitation from the absolute to manifestation? God is behind, in and through the world. God is also the Supreme Being redeeming the world by grace. We cannot account for the world but we can understand its nature which is a process of becoming as a result of tension between opposing forces. If we go above the realm of manifest forms we find only pure Being. If we go below the lowest existent thing in creation we find pure Being. In between we have something which the senses can perceive.

To understand the true nature of life is to overcome the world and is the purpose of the spiritual life. To see through the sense of illusion with the eye of intuition to that which is eternally real and changeless is our goal. When we accomplish this we become knowers of truth and we are free.

The first product of the interaction of dual currents flowing from Spirit is the appearance of a subtle medium of consciousness which contains within it the seed ideas or pictures from which all else is extended. Here is the past, present and future residing in the Now. When these pictures are projected upon the screen of time and space, the worlds are formed, teeming with life and frantic activity. The Supreme Reality thus comes into manifestation through Its own magical power. Thoughts produce all outward forms and the forms are sustained by thoughts. As the pictures on a screen are caused by light shining through the moving film, on which the images are fixed, so the activity of the universe is projected from the Source through fixed images which change not. The images remain but the movement of life causes different projections. It is not necessary for one to fully understand this phenomenon all at once. As we contemplate the nature of the Ultimate Reality more and more light dawns until, in time, all is known. This is the promise of all who stand in the recognition of Truth.

The fabric of nature, termed *maya* by the Hindus, is the substance which God uses to mold the worlds. Everything is formed of the same basic substance and caused to manifest by the Divine Intelligence. "All things were made by him and without him was not made anything that was made." God is the only reality and appears variously so that the cosmic drama might exist.

When the soul, individualized Spirit, is thrown into involvement with nature it becomes so identified with nature that it loses its ability to intuitively perceive the truth about itself. This is termed the *fall of man* or *original sin*. Sin means a darkening or clouding of the mind and perception. Being identified with nature and having its spiritual vision clouded, the soul is deluded and therefore suffers pain and frustration. This delusion is not the result of any mistakes made by the soul. It is a matter of wrong identification. The soul, identified with nature, forgets its divine origin and wanders in the relative worlds until it becomes awakened once more.

God and nature are mutually interdependent. Nature is the production of the divine will and therefore is under its direction. But, nature is necessary for creation to come into manifestation in the first place. In some scriptures God is referred to as Father or the positive pole and nature is referred to as Mother, the negative pole. In these references, positive and negative have nothing to do with good and evil but merely designate the opposite electrical poles necessary for creation to manifest.

The average person seems to have mastered the material world, his vital existence and, to a degree, the workings of the mind. But, he has not yet moved into the awareness of the illumined consciousness. Man awakens from the mortal dream through material consciousness, awareness of mind, the use of intellect or the power of discrimination and, eventually into the awareness of Divine Life. This progressive self-enlargement is the impulse of nature. It cannot be denied. The purpose for man is that he ultimately awaken to the full realization of immortality so that the Divine Consciousness can freely express through and as him.

The Divine dwells in man at the inmost core and cannot ever be obscured. It is the inner light, that which endures and moves from physical birth to physical birth, untouched by death or corruption. The soul awakens from incarnation to incarnation, eventually transcends the ego and becomes aware of pure spiritual existence. Until this happens the soul is destined to experience appearance and disappearance in this world.

We are, in the physical expression, a combination of many traits. We partake of the forces that work in the material world. Our intellectual nature produces self-consciousness which leads us to the place where we see ourselves as being apart from nature. As we unfold we gain a sense of individuality which frees us from dependence upon groups. At times we seem to face the world alone. We do not wish to conform to the social standard. We long to find our true place in life and be involved, yet with a higher purpose. At times we feel helpless and an overwhelming sense of desperation and the grip of anxiety comes over us. The battle begins. We must not be false to ourselves and we must, at the same time, get along with others in this world. By unfolding our spiritual nature we learn to gain a new kind of relationship with the world in which we live and we grow into the awareness of freedom where our integrity is not compromised. This enables us to become aware of ourselves as spiritual entities, living in harmony with outer rules but directed by the internal authority of Divine guidance at all times.

No two people are exactly alike; yet, at the core, we are all the same. The One is expressing as billions of souls on this planet, wearing many outer disguises. No life repeats another but there is a current of sameness which runs through all lives. This is a great mystery to be contemplated. Regardless of the form and pattern we assume, we will one day transcend it *and this process will continue until we reach the clear realization of Absolute Being.* When the soul is lost in identification with this world, it is bound. When it awakens and allows illumination to transform the false nature, the personality, it is freed. *By using discrimination to discern the difference between the Real and the appearance, we attain liberation.*

The major problem facing every man is the integration of his personality and the unfoldment of his divine nature so that the spiritual principle has mastery over all of the activities of life. There is a vital unity of body and soul in man. We need not concern ourselves with erasing human nature; we are to transform it by letting the feed-down of Light and Power have Its way.

Our responsibility is to choose the good; that which leads to self-realization, and train ourselves to be oblivious of the opposite; that which causes bondage and pain. This is why renunciation is so important. Renunciation is the conscious act of discarding dependence upon externals and relying upon the Infinite Invisible at all times and in all places and conditions. The shifting tides of feeling and emotion no longer touch us when we stand in the recognition of the true Self. The egotistical man, the one who believes himself to be separate from God, is an automaton, confined in a psychical and social distortion. The way out of darkness is into the Light. The way out of bondage is into the realization of freedom, which comes as a result of utter dependence upon the Supreme. Liberation is a return to the realization of the soul nature, which is God individualized. Bondage is enslavement to the world without.

The world is not fulfilling a prearranged plan in a mechanical manner. The purpose of creation is the awakening of souls who work consciously in tune with the Infinite Will or who are ever about their "Father's business". Our responsibility is to shake off our confused behavior patterns and adjust our lives in harmony with the Divine plan.

There are certain things over which we have no conscious control. We do not consciously select our parents or our life condition for the early years on earth. This is determined subconsciously by our inner conditionings or karmic patterns, which are the result, for the most part, of past unconscious thoughts, conditionings and feelings. Our ancestry, heredity and environment is determined for us from a subconscious level. But, subject to these limitations we have freedom of choice. We may not have consciously set up the rules for the game of life in which we are presently involved but we certainly have the freedom to make the best of it. With awakened understanding we can learn to cooperate with the forces of nature and not act blindly, on instincts alone.

Even when we act in a seeming spontaneous manner we are often chagrined to find that we are merely acting out suggestions given to us in moments past, when we were not aware. So, at times we are really dramatizing according to hypnotic suggestions, which we received unconsciously. We find that we are not living our true life at all but the life pattern of another. We often find, upon reflection, that we have been acting according to popular opinion, or to the decree of authority. Freedom does not mean compulsive and reckless behavior. *It means to function from the awareness of the inmost Self at all times.*

The way out of the maze of conflicting opinion and theory is the way of the saints and sages; the act of moving into the awareness of pure Being, which alone assures us of freedom.

In this book you will find not only the philosophy, but the system, or way, to freedom. A rational philosophy must be many sided in order to meet the needs of various phases of soul unfoldment and different degrees of personality development.

Every man, from time to time, feels a sense of insufficiency as he becomes aware of the transcience and precariousness of human experience. Those who live on the surface of life may not feel this distress and may not feel the urge to seek realization of the true Self. Like animals; they are born, they mate and they pass away. Awakened people are aware of the inner conflict and seek the solution to life's great mysteries.

At the beginning of the spiritual quest we often find our mind to be clouded, our convictions unsettled and our whole consciousness confused. We do not know which way to turn. There comes a time for all of us when everything we can do for ourselves fails, when we sink into the abyss of darkness and despair, when we would give all for just one gleam of light, one sign that the

Divine Intelligence had a plan and a purpose for us. When we are suppressed by a sense of doubt, denial, despair of life, we can escape only when the grace of God becomes apparent in our lives. Strange as it may seem, the sense of insufficiency and loneliness is due to the working of God; That which is controlling all things. The religious impulse awakens and inspires idealism and supreme fulfillment. Our true nature emerges and enables us to transcend all limitation.

Now, how is the goal of spiritual perfection to be attained? The world is nothing more than the ebb and flow of continual becoming. At the human level all action is caused by personal desire for change. The average person, however, being deluded, does not know what is best for himself and therefore tends to create ever-new complex situations out of which he has to be taken. The only way out of misery-producing, selfish desiring is to awaken to the realization of the Ultimate Truth. Now, the realization of the Ultimate Truth, or wisdom, is not a matter of learning or beliefs. It is a matter of intuitional awakening, which leads to clear realization of the nature of life.

As souls we are naturally aware, at one level, of all the truth there is. So, on the spiritual path we are not concerned with learning through experience, or building a condition of God-consciousness. *Realization is the natural result of our success in clearing the mind and consciousness of all debris and false believing.* It is always present, it has but to be revealed. Stilling of the mind, surrendering the self, results in illumination. Then do we become aware that we are Life and Light.

We can realize perfection in three different ways; *direct perception of the Infinite, through divine love or by subjecting our personal will to the Divine.* These three ways are set forth because we recognize the intellectual, the emotional and the practical aspects of man and we must consider them all. Some men are naturally reflective or inwardly directed. Others are emotional and their feeling nature is pronounced. Still others are active types. At the end, in the final realization, wisdom, love and action are intermingled. Man should aim for the integral life of Spirit. Intuition, feeling and will are different aspects of the soul nature.

Scientific knowledge prepares us for the higher wisdom which is beyond the grasp of the most astute scientific mind. Such knowledge dispells false concepts from the mind of man. But, for knowing the Truth we require rebirth, an intuitional awakening. We must have divine sight. As we persist in the quest for higher knowledge, we find ourselves lifted out of narrow limitations in the pursuit of universal principles of existence. Realization sought for the sake of power, name or fame does not take us far on the spiritual path. *Our urge must be for the realization of Truth for Truth's sake alone.*

To work for liberation we must accept three concepts; the *soul* which is falsely identified with nature, *nature* itself and God, the Supreme Reality which releases us from bondage. Throughout creation we find the three tendencies in nature; lightness, movement and heaviness which appear through the mental qualities as goodness, passion and dullness. The deluded soul is at the mercy of these tendencies but the free soul is above them.

We might as well face the problem of evil head-on. What men term evil is nothing more than the soul's involvement with nature and the tendencies in nature which cause the soul to be deluded and misdirected. When the soul is involved with the tendency toward *heaviness* in nature we say it is evil or malicious; selfish and completely deluded. When the soul is involved with *movement* we say it is *good* or moving toward the Light.

The average man knows only a portion of his true nature, his surface mentality and feelings. There is much beneath the surface of which he knows next to nothing, though it does affect his behavior. We are at times completely overcome by our emotional nature and our reason is cast to the four winds. An insane person is a complete slave while most of us weather the storm and maintain some semblance of normalcy. Under the stress of emotions, we often say or do things which we later regret. Our references to "He is not himself", "He is beside himself", etc., are indications of our realization of this fact. When strong emotions are awakened, we become suggestible and wild ideas overtake us. Ordinarily, the subconscious works with the conscious and we are not aware of the existence of the former; but, if we become possessed of subconscious influences we feel the full force. Unless we have complete self-awareness, we can never attain mastery of life. *Body, life and mind must be integrated*. The average person makes many compromises and lives a life of "quiet desperation". As long as we are tempted to veer from the path which leads to Self-realization we are not free. But, an initiate's life is always one of challenge, which he can see through and overcome.

As we develop pure intentions and control our selfish motivations, we find that the awareness of Life Eternal is coming to the surface of our consciousness. In deep stillness we experience the awareness of God and we find rest from earthly involvement. Thus, insight is born. The Self-realized soul shall never perish . . . he knows his true identity.

We all need to seek God. We all need to yearn for the realization of the True Self. This is sure. We need to surrender ourselves completely in order to *forget* our limiting beliefs so that we can *remember* our God-nature. This is the great secret which leads to Self-realization. When we are able to do this we find a transformation taking place, all error is discarded and the light and purity of God is made manifest. We need not concern ourselves with whether or not we are worthy. We are; because we are individualizations of Spirit. This is enough.

None of us, of ourselves, can become free from involvement with this world. We do not know how to extricate ourselves. But, reliance upon the Infinite awakens us and lifts us above mundane attachments. This movement of Life is termed the *grace of God*. We are all destined for heaven; for liberation and Self-realization. None can escape it. Surrender of self-will in favor of Divine Will is the obligation of all who would become enlightened. What else is there but God? What else is there but God's will?

In the beginning we all have a problem. Shall we become involved with the world or shall we retreat from it? Since we are already involved, the only conclusion we can come to is to act in the world with the proper mental attitude, a positive one. We are, while in this world, to be fully involved, *but we are to be anchored in the realization of our True Nature as God*. When we find our right place in the scheme of things and we work with the attitude that the Divine is working through us we are released from bondage. It is that simple. So simple that many overlook it. We are not here for ourselves but we are here for the good of the world. While we are in the world we are required to work selflessly and redeem it. This ideal gives us much to ponder and reflect upon. What is the true nature of God? What is our true nature. What does the Divine Intelligence wish to do through and as me?

Laziness is not freedom. Nor is selfish action. The important thing is our attitude and our motivation for what we do. We are, to the best of our ability, to build a world which is wholesome and upon which we can base a life of Divine aspiration. With a firm foundation we can more easily find time for higher thoughts and reflections. When we act in the spirit of dedication and detachment, doing what must be done in this world, we are preparing for what is to come. It is our duty to work in this manner.

When we work with the consciousness of the Divine working through us we are not attached to what we do. We take things as they come and we leave them without regret. God finds in us, a clear channel for the fulfilling of His will. Karma can be transcended when we work consciously in tune with the Divine will. The more we throw ourselves into the awareness of pure Being, into the nature of God, the greater is our personal freedom.

Now, while it is true that all personal action is, in the highest sense, a waste of time as far as God-realization is concerned; while we are here we are condemned to some form of behavior. What we must do is try our best to engage in action which is for the overall good of man. When we are in tune, the Universal Intelligence works through our intellect, mind and body to fulfill the Ultimate Aim for all life. Some men lose themselves in the activities of the world. Others withdraw and become escapists. The ideal man works in the world for the good of all and maintains his awareness of Self. He is in the world but *not of it*. He wears the world as a loose garment and is eternally free.

God alone is the ruler of the worlds and the dispenser of grace. For God's will must all work be done. The rules by which man lives must be obeyed because there is a purpose for them. These rules are not ends in themselves but the final goal is assured for all who abide by them. This is the way the universe works.

The goal of ultimate realization is finally realized when all souls are God-conscious. Then duality disappears and only the awareness of Oneness exists. This is a condition beyond all tendencies and qualities. One who realizes this while yet embodied is a master, a free soul. We are to see the transformation of our human nature into the law and power of the Divine. We are to be inspired by pure knowledge and moved by Divine will. Our purified nature is to be assimilated into the Divine substance. We are to realize the nature of God. Our body, mind and spirit, the conscious, subconscious and unconscious then work together in rhythm and joy. We are to be transformed and redeemed. We are to be made pure and become the pattern through which the Divine Light is effortlessly expressed. Our activities are for the good of the world. We take upon ourselves the redemption of mankind. We cannot cease from our work until all souls are awakened and know the truth even as we know it. Our efforts, example and illumination lead mass consciousness to the real end and purpose of creation. Anchored in timelessness, aware of the Eternal, we work not for ourselves but for the others. We become God in action.

Then will the purpose for creation be fulfilled and it will be on earth as it is in heaven.

CHAPTER ONE

The Totality of Being

The Totality of Being

Much of the material in this text is, of necessity, repetitive. The reason for this is to interconnect all facets of the teaching and to provide an opportunity for the serious student of truth to contemplate the nature of Reality and thereby awaken spiritually.

God is the only Real Substance in the universe. When the nature of God is understood, man knows all there is to know about the nature of life. He knows how and why creation came forth, his relationship to it and his certain destiny. In short, man becomes a knower of Truth and the result is freedom.

Prophets of all lands and ages who have succeeded in their quest for knowledge have become enlightened and have realized directly the Supreme Reality behind the forms of creation. Their wisdom and spiritual counsel have become the scriptures of the world. Through them we find the same basic truths and the way to realize these truths as a personal experience. There is but one method by which the world, internal and external, has evolved. In this book I have lifted the veil which has for so long obscured the truth from the vision of people. You will note, as you read, that the basic principles are those which underlie all religions. Indeed, it is as it has been described, "like pearls on a string, so do the various religions appear, with the thread of truth running through them all".

Man possesses never-ending faith and believes intuitively in the existence of a Substance, of which the objects of sense; hearing, touch, sight, taste and smell are but properties. As man identifies himself with a material body composed of the ingredients of nature, he is able to perceive and comprehend the physical world only and not the real Substance from which the things of the world are formed. Because the average man is sense-bound, he cannot comprehend the subtle nature of God unless he becomes spiritually awakened and becomes aware of his own divine nature. This is the meaning of the words, "When you have lifted up the Son of man, then shall you know that I am He." Without this awakening, without this clearing of human consciousness, the Ultimate Truth can never be known. We may be decent, law abiding citizens, possessed of religious convictions and motivated by high ideals; but without spiritual awakening the inner secrets will never be clearly comprehended.

THE TRUE NATURE OF GOD

Here is the truth of the matter; *God is both transcendental, above the time-order and all of creation and, at the same time, God is actively manifesting through and as all creation.* (Study carefully, the chart included with this chapter.)

You see, Spirit is pure Being, with no conditionings. It just *Is*. Spirit can be experienced but not known because for something to be known there must be a knower and that which is known. When we experience pure Being we are not conscious of any sense of separation. But, God can be known. *What we call God is really the first outward manifestation or self-modification of Spirit.* God is perceived as a triune Substance. Here we find a partial modification of Spirit as Existence; we find Divine Magnetism as Consciousness and we find Force as Power. Christian mystics refer to these aspects of God as the Trinity; Father (Existence), Son (the positive aspect or Universal Intelligence) and the Holy Ghost ("sacred vibration" or movement which carries creation into expression).

Because man is an individualization of all that God is, man can, by turning his attention inward, learn to clearly perceive for himself the true nature of God. He can comprehend his real nature as existence, consciousness and bliss.

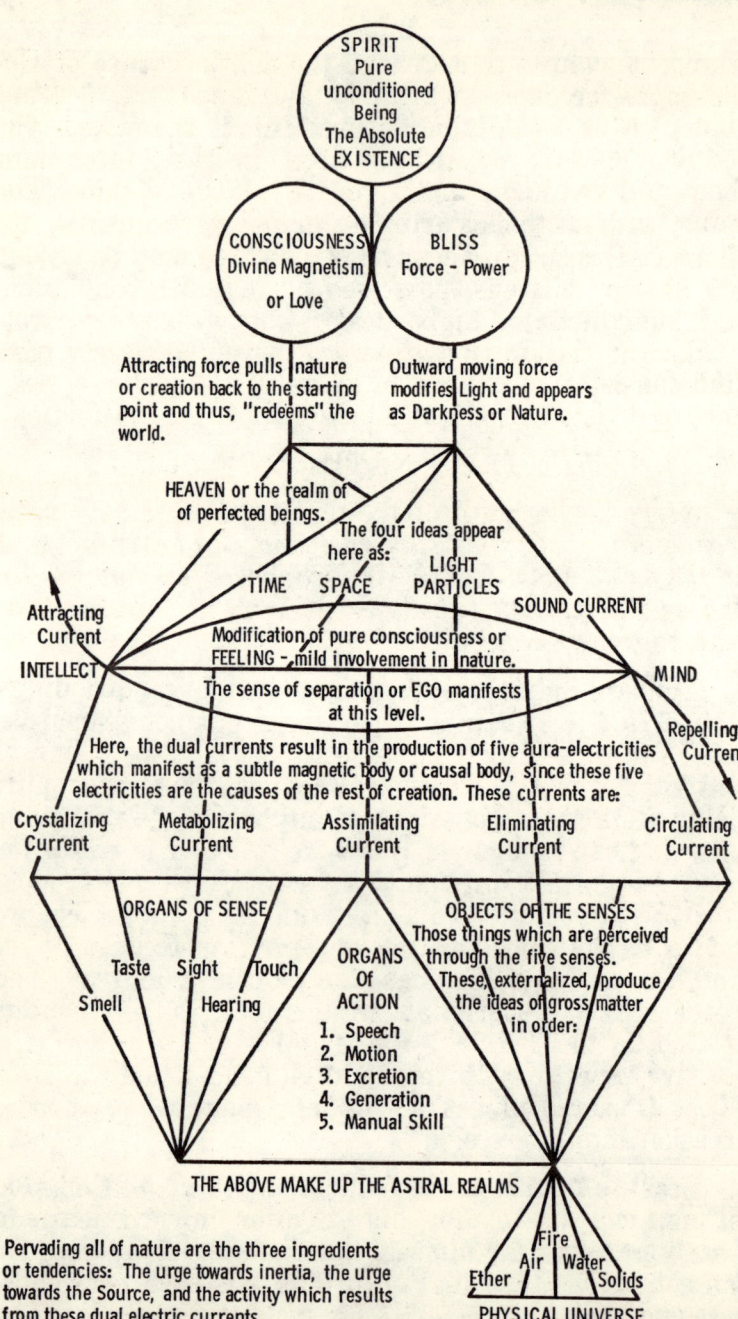

THE TOTALITY OF BEING

The manifestation of Omnipotent Force (and its complementary expression, Divine Magnetism) is a vibration which can be intuitively heard as a sound. This sound is verbally approximated as *Amen*, by Christians, *Aum* or *Om* by Hindus and as *Hum* by Tibetens. This is the Cosmic Sound or the *Word*. "In the beginning was the Word and the Word was with God and the Word was God."

This vibration is composed of four aspects. In it we find the sense of change or, time. We find the appearance of division or, space. Then, there are light particles. These four components; *force, time, space and light particles, make up all of nature*. The Word, manifesting or *becoming flesh* resulted in creation. Therefore, we see that creation is really God appearing *as* creation on all levels; as the burning power is inseparable from the fire and as the wave is inseparable from the ocean. ("All things were made by Him; and without Him was not anything made that was made . . . and the Word was made flesh and dwelt among us").

These manifestations of God, moving in the direction of creation, are called, altogether, the *Darkness* because a soul identified with them cannot comprehend the Light of Truth. Becoming identified with these manifestations, a person becomes confused and deluded. When man awakens and clearly understands the nature of Darkness he comprehends it so clearly that he is able to rise above it and he also comprehends the nature of God, as being transcendental and as manifest at the same time. These four divisions of the Word are referred to in the Bible as the four beasts, with an inner and outer nature. "And in the midst of the throne, and around about the throne, were four beasts full of eyes before and behind."

The manifestation of Divine Magnetism is the same as Universal (Christ) Consciousness and shining on the aspects making up the Darkness (force, time, space and light particles) tends to attract creation to Itself. So, we have a dual manifestation; the outward flowing force which carries creation into manifestation and the attracting power which tends to draw creation back to Itself. This attracting power is evident in all creation. It is Light and Life. "In him was Life, and the Life was the Light of men." "And the Light shineth in Darkness and the Darkness comprehended it not."

In the initial movement towards creation, the outer reflection of spiritual rays are termed *Sons of God*. When these rays are further involved with the Darkness and as a result, lose the awareness of their true nature and become deluded or darkened, the sense of ego or separation appears and then the Son of God becomes the Son of Man. In order to be free we must awaken from identification with the Darkness and once again become consciously aware of our Divine nature. We must turn the attention back to the Source and *remember* our true nature.

Becoming further involved, the Son of Man or, soul, finds that the magnetic field surrounding him becomes polarized. The positive pole is the faculty of discrimination and enables a person to determine the difference between Truth and appearances. The negative pole is the mind, the creative medium through which the soul creates in the world. Being led by feeling, the soul which is deluded, tends to use the mind to create further complications for itself. However, the mind used with discrimination can be a useful tool for putting order in the world.

As the soul *descends,* five aura-electricities are produced in its magnetic field. (See chart). The production of these five aura-electricities results in a magnetic field which is called the Causal body of the soul (The Son of God) composed of these five root-causes.

Electricities are evolved from the polarized magnetic field and are endowed with the three electric attributes; the positive, the negative and the neutralizing. The positive attributes of these five electricities are the organs of senses, in subtle form; smell, taste, sight, touch and hearing. The neutralizing attributes of these five electricities are the organs of action; excretion, generation, speech, motion and the exercise of manuel dexterity. The negative attributes of these five electricities become the objects of desire. These fifteen attributes, with dual polarity, plus Mind, Intelligence, Ego and Feeling make up the fine material body of the soul which is composed of life force or energy. This is the body that survives physical death and the blueprint around which the physical body is formed.

A further extension results in the appearance of gross matters, which are a reflection of the five objects of the senses and they appear as solids, liquids, fiery, gaseous and ethereal substances. These form the material body of the soul and appear, in the larger sense, as the material world. The fifteen attributes, along with the five gross reflections and Mind, Intelligence, Feeling and Ego constitute the twenty-four principles or Elders, as mentioned in the Book of Revelations (5:4). "And around about the throne were four and twenty seats; and upon the seats I saw four and twenty Elders."

These twenty-four principles complete the full manifestation of the Darkness and are really modifications of Light for the purpose of appearing as creation. Therefore, all of creation is a play of ideas on the Eternal, never-changing Substance, which is God.

THE SEVEN PLANES OF EXISTENCE

Commencing from God, down to the gross material plane, there are seven different planes or spheres.

1. *God* — No man can fully comprehend this level unless he sheds his illusions; then he can know it.
2. *The Sphere of The Holy Spirit* — This is inaccessible to all but the fully illumined. It is the first movement in the direction of creation.

3. *The Plane of Spiritual Reflection* — Here we find the realm where the idea of separate existence takes place; this is the realm of the Sons of God. No one in Darkness can comprehend it.

4. *The Beginning of The Creation of Darkness* — This is the connecting link and the *door* between material creation and spiritual reality.

5. *The Sphere of Magnetic Auras* — Here we find the subtle blueprint for all that is to come. This is the causal realm.

6. *The Sphere of Elecric Attributes* — A more dense manifestation, the astral realms.

7. *The Sphere of Gross Material Creation*—This level is visible to the average person.

As man is God, in reflection, so is the body of man an exact replica of the universe. In the physical body of man we find seven vital centers which are located in the spine. Man can, by turning inward, move along the spinal pathway and perceive the inner light at the different levels of unfoldment. The seven centers of vital force correspond to the seven spheres or planes.

A full explanation of these vital centers in the body will be given later in this text. The seven planes or spheres and the seven vital places in the body of man are the fourteen distinguishable stages of creation.

THE FIVE COVERINGS OF THE SOUL

When involved in nature, the soul has five coverings which can be clearly described.

1. The first covering is a sheath composed of ego, the sense of separation; Intelligence the faculty of discrimination; Mind the creative medium and Feeling, as a result of consciousness. This covering is perceived consciously in deep meditation and unconsciously in deep, dreamless sleep, as bliss.

THE TOTALITY OF BEING

2. The second covering is a result of the projection of magnetic auras from Intelligence and this is termed the Seat of Knowledge.
3. The third covering is a projection of the magnetic field known as the Mind. This forms the mental body.
4. The fourth covering is the body of life-force or energy, the astral body.
5. The fifth and final covering is the physical body. These five coverings result in the appearance of creation on a cosmic scale and the appearance of man on a smaller scale.

When we drop the physical body we function in the astral body on the astral or energy planes. When we drop the astral body we function as Mind in the mental realms. In time, all coverings are stripped away and the soul becomes aware of its true nature and experiences the realization of Oneness.

Frequent study of this first chapter will clarify the explanations to be found in the following text.

CHAPTER TWO

Genesis Unveiled

Genesis Unveiled

Creation is sent forth as the inner urge of God and results in *movement*. The outflowing force, on the negative pole, carries creation into full manifestation. The Darkness is everywhere present but not yet formed.

When this is completed, the action of the positive pole, the Magnetic Attraction, begins to influence creation. Light particles are brought together and take ethereal, gaseous, fiery, liquid and solid forms. In this way the suns, planets and moons appear.

In due time, because of the influence of this Magnetic Attraction, sometimes referred to as Divine Love, the outer coatings of Spirit are withdrawn. With the partial withdrawal of the first covering, the vegetable kingdom appears. Life and vitality begin to manifest. A partial withdrawal of the next covering results in the appearance of the animal kingdom. When the coverings are withdrawn sufficiently so that the body of intelligence is revealed, the soul gains conscious ability to know right from wrong; it develops discrimination. Hence, rational man comes on the scene. When the next to the last covering is withdrawn, man becomes aware of the existence of his Divine Nature. *When the final covering is withdrawn, man realizes himself as Spirit and remembers his nature as a Son of God.* Entering into the ocean of Light, he becomes eternally free.

> "In the beginning God created the heaven and the earth. And the earth was without form and void; and Darkness was upon the face of the deep. And the Spirit of God moved upon the face of the waters. And God said, Let there be light; and there was light. And God saw the light, that it was good; and God divided the light from the Darkness." Genesis 1:1-4.

First came the Darkness or the full projection of the the fabric of nature. Then, Magnetic Attraction began to influence this formless void and light appeared.

Elements refers to the components of the Darkness from which things were formed. The dual flow of electric currents appeared as heaven—the World of Reality; the earth—Darkness or the form building medium. But, at this stage the Darkness had no form. It was ready for the creative act. With the influence of the Magnetic Attraction the process of creation began. Spirit and Nature, Light and Darkness interact and the invisible begins to become visible.

> "And God called the light day, and the darkness he called night. And the evening and the morning were the first day." 1:5.

The Light is the Eternal Day which forever shines. It is the realm to which we all aspire. The Darkness or first subtle expression of nature is night or, delusion. Here, the dual aspects of Spirit set the stage for what is to come. The unfoldment of creation takes place in *time*: and time is one of the four basic units of the Darkness. Divided by segments each stage took millions of years to unfold.

> "And God said, Let there be firmament in the midst of the waters, and let it divide the waters from the waters. And God made the firmament, and divided the waters which were under the firmament from the waters which were above the firmament, and it was so. And God called the firmament heaven. And the evening and the morning were the second day." -1:6-8.

This marked the completion of the building of the inner, subtle realms. Definite lines of division were laid out as magnetic fields, marking off planes and spheres. Waters, means various manifestations of consciousness.

> "And God said, let the waters under the heavens be gathered together unto one place, and let dry land appear: and it was so. And God called the dry land earth; and the gathering together of the waters he called sea: and God saw that it was good. And God said, let the earth bring forth grass, the herb yielding seed, and the fruit tree yielding fruit after his kind, whose seed is in

itself, after his kind: and God saw that it was good.
And the evening and the morning were the third day."
-1:9-13.

The concealed vitality began to come forth as the vegetable kingdom. Definite images in Cosmic Mind began to emerge as the different kinds of plants, capable of reproducing their kind.

"And God said, Let there be lights in the firmament of the heaven to divide the day from the night; and let them be for signs and seasons, and for days and years: And let them be for lights in the firmament of heaven to give light upon the earth: and it was so. And God made two great lights; the greater to rule the day and the lesser light to rule the night: he made the stars also. And God set them in the firmament of the heaven to give light upon the earth. And to rule over the day and over the night, to divide the light from the darkness: and God saw that it was good. And the evening and the morning were the fourth day." -1:14-19.

During this day or, cycle, order was established in the solar system. The planets settled into movements in relationship to each other. All of nature, from the lowest to the highest, works together for good; or that the Divine Plan might unfold. As we go along we shall see how man himself is attuned to all of nature due to the electrical activity in the universe.

"And God said, Let the waters bring forth abundantly the moving creature that hath life, and the fowl that may fly above the earth in the open firmament of heaven. And God created great whales, and every living creature that moveth, which the waters of the earth brought forth abundantly, after their own kind, and every winged fowl after his kind: and God saw that it was good. And God blessed them saying, Be fruitful and multiply, and fill the waters of the sea, and let the fowl multiply in the earth. And the evening and the morning were the fifth day." -1:20-23.

Due to the Magnetic Attraction the organs of sense were revealed resulting in the appearance of living forms. The redemption of the worlds began with the appearance of the planets because this was when the Attracting Force began to pull the gross Darkness back to Itself; to the original condition, as it was before the initial act of creation. Redemption started then, eons ago, and has been continuing ever since.

> "And God said, Let the earth bring forth the living creature after his kind, the cattle, and the creeping things, the beast of the earth, after his kind: and it was so. And God made the beast of the earth, after his kind, the cattle after his kind, and everything that creepeth upon the earth after his kind: and God saw that it was good."   -1:24-25.

The animals appeared and learned to adapt to their environment. The inner urge to survive resulted in a modification of the species. But, the species were determined from the beginning. They brought forth after their kind. There is no evidence that there was a change from one species to another. The seed-ideas or blueprints existed from the beginning and made their appearance when conditions were suitable.

In plants we see the capacity to trap energy by the process of photosynthesis and in animals we see a further evolution in that they, unlike plants, can move from point to point in space. Animals eat plants which have trapped the energy and take energy into their bodies in this manner. Some animals devour other animals. Animals live by instinct and their subconscious minds are programmed as a result of their efforts to adapt to their environment. Animals might be termed "energy-converters" of plants or animals and thus the energy is transferred. They learn, by experience, to survive and these instinctive survival patterns are transmitted to their offspring.

> "So God created man in his own image, in the image of God created he him; male and female created he them. And God blessed them, and God said unto them, Be fruitful and multiply and replenish the earth, and subdue it: and have dominion over the fish of the sea,

> and over the fowl of the air, and over every living thing that moveth upon the face of the earth. And God said, Behold I have given you every herb bearing seed, which is upon the face of the earth, and every tree, in which is the fruit of the tree yielding seed: to you it shall be for meat. And to every beast of the earth, and to every fowl of the air, and to every thing that creepeth upon the earth, wherein there is life, I have given green herbs for meat: and it was so. And God saw everything that he had made, and, behold, it was very good. And the evening and the morning were the sixth day."   -1:27-31.

Now we see the stage being set for the appearance of man on the planet. You will notice that in every step of the process, that which was necessary for the maintenance of life for higher forms, when they came on the scene, was provided before they appeared. First came vegetation: food for animals. The Divine Plan always works things out in orderly sequence. At this stage the pattern for man was set in Divine Mind, ready to emerge. And, true to the pattern, man was created as male and female, positive and negative, according to the dual flow of force.

> "Thus the heavens and the earth were finished, and all the host of them. And on the seventh day God ended his work which he had made; and he rested on the seventh day from all his work which he had made." 2:1-2.

The time had come for the emergence of human beings. This point is critical to us as it marks the beginning of the most important step in the creative process.

> "But there went up a mist from the earth, and watered the whole face of the ground. And the Lord God formed man of the dust of the ground, and breathed into his nostrils the breath of life: and man became a living soul. And the Lord God planted a garden eastward in Eden: and there he put the man whom he had formed."   -2:6-8.

In ancient occult history we read of the time when man was new on the planet and the planet was covered with a mist or fog. Where did man come from? How was it possible for him to appear?

Man appeared quite naturally as a result of the pull of the powerful Magnetic Attraction. Just as when the veil is lifted a bit, exposing the organs of action, plants emerge; and as the exposure of the organs of sense results in the appearance of animals; so, *the unveiling of the covering of intelligence results in the appearance of man*. Man, because he can discriminate, because he is self-conscious, can determine the course of his own evolution. He can decide to work in harmony with the laws of the universe which leads to freedom or he can decide to continue in an endless round of unreasoned activity. He has a choice to make.

When, over a great period of time, the awakening souls which were expressing through animal bodies needed a more refined vehicle through which to express, nature saw to it that one was prepared.

Some teach that man was a special act of creation. Are we to suppose that the bodies of the first man and woman suddenly materialized? It would seem that since all other life forms, up to this point appeared in logical sequence, that man's appearance was similarly in line with Divine Order.

THE FALL OF MAN

The fall of man is the descent of the soul into Darkness, the fabric of nature, through layers of ever-more-dense consciousness. We have, in a sense, all fallen from grace. That is, souls now embodied have lost sight of their spiritual natures. But you and I are not embodied because of any transgression made by anyone else who preceded us on this planet. We are embodied either because we were thrown into total involvement with Darkness from the beginning or because we, out of curiosity, became involved. *Original* sin is the first covering of our Divine Nature. This is what sin means: a covering or darkening of the spiritual nature for some reason or another.

Why does man fall into involvement with nature? There are two reasons; he becomes involved because he is unconsciously thrown forth into the Darkness initially, and has to awaken slowly, through various life-forms, incarnation after incarnation; or, if he is only partially deluded in the beginning and allows his feeling nature and curiosity to lead him astray, he becomes involved, deluded and trapped, forgetting his way back to paradise.

Man can lose his way for any number of reasons; a thirst for power, a desire for sensation, or just for the sake of experiencing on grosser levels. Wherever his attention flows and he becomes identified; from that point of view he looks out upon the world. Not all of us have come up through the myriad life-forms over millions of years of striving. Some of us "fell" into involvement to our present level from a more rarified sphere, because we were curious. A few enlightened beings, now on earth, are here because they want to help others find their way out of darkness into the clear light of Self-knowledge. Since awakening souls need bodies in order to express in this world at their level of unfoldment, human bodies were formed, and, they brought forth after their kind, in order that others in the ascending scale might have a way out. In the human body we find the highly refined nervous system and brain through which Intelligence can express. The human body is, therefore, a necessity in the chain of events.

So, there are two orders of souls; one group which fell into involvement, unconsciously, with the initial creative urge and; the other group which dwelt in the Kingdom of Reality, the True Heaven, of which this world is but a reflection. The general order of experience is freedom and God-consciousness. Among the former group, the souls found expression through mineral, plant and animal forms before awakening as man.

Because one group started out more deeply involved and more deluded than the other does not make one group more favored than the other. It is all God's impersonal drama. It is the way of creation. But, the pattern of human experience must be different from group to group. Some souls, now on this planet, did not come up through animal forms . . . and others did. The former group, those who "fell" to this level from a once conscious realization of God, have a dim memory of how it was before they began to dream this dream of mortality. "Remember, therefore from whence thou art fallen and repent." (Rev. 2:5).

The practice of Divine remembering is the most effective form of meditation for this group of souls. How could you remember how it was if you had not fallen from a condition of near-perfection? The only way out of the dream is to awaken. To remain in the dream and try to fathom its meaning and significance is frustrating because the dream itself is the result of ignorance. We cannot know Reality while in a deluded condition. One might, over a period of time, by using discrimination, discount everything God is not, and arrive at what God is, but it is doubtful that this is an effective route to freedom. The fastest way to Self-realization is to cast the attention into the Infinite and be swept along by the mighty Attracting Current which pulls everything back to the pure unconditioned state, as it was "before the world was".

Adam is representative of the first human group on the planet. We do not speak of one man and one woman. We refer to the group which evolved on this planet and became ready for spiritual awakening. Up until this time, the groups lived much as animals, in a dream-state, with the sense of reason beginning to emerge. They lived instinctively and did not know good from evil.

To them, good was that which meant survival. Evil was that which was non-survival. The idea of good and evil is ever in relationship to goals and determined by our level of understanding. Whatever we do, think or feel which clouds our vision of Truth, is evil. Good and evil are included in the basic fabric of nature. Dual forces are always in creation, but these forces are not at war with each other. Darkness, heaviness, gravity; is evil . . . or that which tends to grossness or materiality. Light and uplifting power, the Attracting Force, is good, or that which tends towards freedom and liberation.

Good—the Attracting Force, will ultimately overcome or redeem evil: the negative repelling force in nature. Without these dual forces in nature creation would not exist. Man overcomes evil (the tendency towards more involvement with Darkness) not by fighting with it, but by attuning himself with the Attracting Power which will, of Itself, lift him into the realization of the Light.

By working in harmony with life-giving laws we rise above this world and enter into heaven, the World of Reality.

The door through which souls enter into self-consciousness is also the door through which they become deluded. In the former instance, in the Genesis story, souls were still in a dreamlike condition, even though embodied in forms similar to what we now know to be human bodies. Gradually, they became aware of their surroundings and began to use their sense of reason. Formerly, when they lived only by instinct, they learned to react to conditions and situations in order to survive. They mated and reproduced, they ate food, found shelter and, as they awakened, formed crude social groups or organizations. The unveiling of the faculty of reason opened their eyes and made them like *gods*, with the ability to think, use intuition, creative imagination and logic. This lifted them above their dependence upon subconscious habit patterns. They could go against the laws of nature. But, they could also transcend themselves. It was a necessary step in their unfoldment.

Man alone can use creative imagination to visualize situations and conditions different from those heretofore experienced, and then, move into them. This enables him to change his world. It enables him to speed up his evolution through concentration. He can discard behavior patterns which do not contribute to his well-being and he can alter circumstances to suit his fancy. Until he reached this point in his unfoldment, man was dependent upon the upward pull of Spirit. At this level, however, he became somewhat independent and could elect either to continue his unfoldment or to become fascinated and involved with the world because of free will. Unfortunately, unenlightened people do not always desire that which is best for them in the long run. Many, even with the sense of reason developed, still act selfishly and, pursuing one glamorous experience after another, become sidetracked.

Awakening man, instead of directing his attention towards further awakening, became fascinated with nature and because of his investigation became confused. Man is, because of his superior knowledge, the one elected to subdue the earth. How many miss the point! We are supposed to work consciously to transform the world and bring the kingdom of heaven on earth. This, of course, is not the ultimate goal, but it gives us something worthwhile to do while we are about the business of realizing the Ultimate Truth.

When man awakened to the level where he was self-conscious he could know death. Before this, the soul moved from the physical body to the astral realms and back into a physical body, with hardly any awareness of the transition. But, with self-consciousness and reason, man could perceive the difference between astral and physical experience. Thus, he could fear the unknown. Death took him away, to an unfamiliar realm.

At this level of unfoldment, man began to till the ground and wear clothing. He began to form groups and plan for his future. He became, in effect, a time-binder. He could think in terms of past, present and future. He could learn from the experiences of others and build upon accumulated knowledge. And, because of his dim memory of his real origin he developed a religious sense and began to ponder the mystery of life.

Before self-consciousness, man was as in a dream, aware of the inner worlds. But afterwards, because of his outward flowing attention, he lost his awareness. He felt alone and "naked". This was part of the Divine Plan for it forced growth.

Throughout the animal kingdom and even in man, we find the manifestation of the dual electric flows. In the male, reason predominates. In the female, feeling is foremost. Feeling can lead man astray. It causes him to seek pleasure in a thousand different directions. Any time that man allows feeling to lead him to seek pleasure, without regard to the consequences, he opens the door to pain and disillusionment. This is why it is important for man to learn to use reason to control his feeling nature.

In dealing with the Adam and Eve story, we must consider the group of souls which were awakening after millions of years of unconscious involvement with nature in lower life forms. Awakening to a sense of self-consciousness, they began to reach out for greater awareness. Looking out through the window of the mind, they began to control circumstances and to create as gods.

The order of souls which were individualized on the positive pole, did not have to become involved with material creation. Some of them, however, did become intrigued with the appearances in nature and lost their way. Remember, the two characteristics of the Darkness is that it is *Truth-veiling* and *form-building*. Involvement with it blinds the soul so that its intuition is suppressed. Some of these once-bright souls fell into the astral realms: others became fully involved with the physical realms. Some actually became involved, as part of the cosmic process, in order to awaken souls and show them the way to freedom. These cosmic benefactors were called angels.

The garden planted "eastward in Eden" is the awareness of bliss and fulfillment experienced by man who is consciously or unconsciously in tune with the Infinite Will. In the body, different parts are assigned geographical positions; South is down into the body; North is the top of the head; West is back of the skull and East is in the forehead where we find the psychic center which is the main connecting point in man between the inner and outer worlds. A man's consciousness centered "eastward" or in the third-eye center, causes him to be in touch with Divine Realms. When man's attention flows in a "westward" or "southward" direction, to the lower brain center and into the body, he loses his intuitive perception and becomes body-bound and sense-bound. He forgets his spiritual nature and thinks himself to be a physical body only, living in a physical world which, to him, is the only reality. Becoming firmly identified with outer things, man forgets how to return, through the "gate" in the East, to Eden, land of fulfillment.

In lower life forms we find that some organisms could reproduce after their own kind without assistance. But, as life forms became more specialized, the sexes were divided into male and female. Males and females need each other, not only for purposes of reproduction, but for the positive-negative electrical interchange resulting from close proximity which tends to neutralize or balance their natures. Mistaken teachings about sex have been the cause of confusion, guilt and inner conflict for millions of people. It has been incorrectly taught that sexual relations are a deterrent to spiritual progress. As long as man has a body he will have the urges of the body to reproduce as nature designed it, and he will always have the urge to commune with his counterpart, the female. Sexual communication is a form of soul communion when the man and woman involved are ideally mated. When this is the case there is a flow of vital forces from one to the other, enhancing the awareness of life, and resulting in an uplift of consciousness. The intelligent approach to sexual communion is not suppression, but proper use of the function with the right mental attitude.

In the scriptures of ancient India, we find the story of the first man and woman, symbolic of the first human beings on the planet. We read of *man born of the creator* and his wife, *true image*. Their children intermarried with perfected beings who could assume corporeal form, and from these first families descended the human race. To prepare a more highly refined body for awakening souls, some of the children born to early men were *from above*. That is, they were souls descending from the astral into the physical in human bodies, without falling lower than human. Two orders of souls, some *from below* and *some from above* met, and produced an upsurge in human evolution. In other words, sleeping souls, making their way up from simple beginnings through repeated rebirths, reached the stage where they were able to communicate with fallen angels; the result being refinement of the cerebro-spinal nervous system of man through which greater awareness could be expressed.

THE SPIRITUAL NATURE OF MAN

"What is man, that thou shouldst magnify him? and that thou shouldst set thine heart upon him? And that thou shouldst visit him every morning and try him every moment?" Job 7:17-18.

"When I consider thy heavens, the work of thy fingers, the moon and the stars, which thou hast ordained; What is man that thou art mindful of him? And the son of man, that thou visitest him? For thou hast made him a little lower than the angels, and hast crowned him with glory and honor. Thou madest him to have dominion over the works of thy hands; thou hast put all things under his feet." Psalms 8:3-6.

Man became involved with nature and he has been on this planet for millions of years. Unawakened man is, for the most part, unconsciously moving through the world, as in a dream. He is acted upon by forces within and without, of which he has little awareness and practically no control. He is born into this world, structures his time for a number of years, occasionally breaks through to the realization of deeper levels of his own consciousness, then dies, to rest a while on the astral level until the subconscious pull of earth causes him to be incarnated once more. Reincarnation is the cycle of necessity. Man, failing to awaken from the mortal dream in one sojourn on earth, must return, time and time again, until he does awaken and come into the realization of his God-nature.

All things in creation are forever interchanging their influences. For instance, astrology, the study of man's response to planetary stimuli, shows how human beings are really tied to distant heavenly bodies on a subtle level. The heavenly bodies, in themselves, possess no harmful or helpful radiations but merely offer a lawful and orderly channel for the outward operation of cause and effect patterns within the subconscious mind of man.

In discussing astrology, I am not suggesting that one become overly concerned with the predictive aspects of the science. Rather, let us examine the workings of nature in order to arrive at a more cosmic understanding of how creation, as an electrical phenomenon, is able to function in an orderly fashion. The unawakened man is at the mercy of environmental influences. The more he awakens and becomes attuned to the Attracting Force, the Divine Center, the less he is influenced. In time, he is able to live by grace, in harmony with life on all levels. He does not have to think about it. It just happens.

A soul incarnates into a flesh body at a time and place when and where his subconscious karmic patterns are in harmony with nature. Thus, it is no accident that you were born when and where you were, to the parents you had and in the early environment which was yours. By setting up a chart a competent astrologer can accurately determine your karmic condition at your time of birth, by analyzing the positions of the planets at that time. This even enables an astrologer to predict how you will tend to react in the future to certain planetary stimuli. Since most people do not make any conscious effort to improve themselves, the horoscope can be a guide to predicting human behavior.

Astrology, along with medicine, mathematics, music and architecture, was one of the great sciences of the ancient world. We know that this science was known to the Chaldeans and also practiced by the Egyptians, Hindus, Chinese, Persians and the leaders of the great civilizations of the Americas. Astrology is divisible into two distinct sciences. The esoteric science deals with the mysteries of the cosmos, the spiritual, intellectual, moral and physical chemistry of the world. It reveals the anatomy and psychology of God. It sets forth an explanation of existence and a moral relationship between things. It reveals the mathematical pattern of creation. It is really a study of celestial dynamics. Exoteric astrology, on the other hand, is the predictive aspect. In this text I am dealing with esoteric or, inner astrology.

We know that man is composed of two parts; the Spirit which animates the body and, the body itself. In order to properly understand astrology, we must understand the nature of man. We must understand the whole of creation, both visible and invisible, that which is seen and that which is unseen.

Pythagoras, who gained his knowledge from the wise men of Egypt, India and Greece, stated that the planets moved about the sun. The ancients were not lacking in wisdom. Enlightened men are ever with us but their wisdom is only offered to the masses when the mass consciousness is receptive to it.

In space there are stars and each star is a sun, and these suns are manifestors of pure energy which sustains the world. Each of the suns has its planets which are reflectors of its energies. These planets not only reflect but they distribute the energies radiating from the suns. Channeled through the planets the energy is converted into positive and negative qualities.

So-called material bodies are composed of energy which has a certain emanational power. The physical energies of these elements are referred to as force and force exercises an influence upon structures which are in proximity to that force. Man on earth receives three kinds of energy; Spiritual energy from the planets, Physical energy reflected from the planets and Elementary energy from the earth on which he resides. Superior forces influence inferior forces. Therefore, lesser forces are acted upon by greater force.

The appearance of plants and organisms was the result of the upward movement of force, as explained earlier (The Attracting Power of God which unveiled Life). And, this force within the forms of earth is also acted upon from without. Spiritual force works through inert material forms and activity results from the interplay of Attractive Force and inertia (gravity). Theologians refer to this activity as the struggle between good and evil; God and the *devil*.

Spirit regulates all of creation through these streams of force. The One Life flows through the suns and is converted and channeled through the planets. Over a period of time, as the result of inner revelation and outer investigation, ancient seers were able to discover the quality of force emanating from certain suns, modified by specific planets. Then, they were able to recognize the relationship of these forces to the behavior of man, as well as to other living things.

The planet earth consists of a physical body with a series of electric and magnetic fields. We are bound to the sun by subtle cords or, lines, of force. It is thought that the earth contains seven electric zones and therefore, seven degrees of density. The number seven is an oft-mentioned number in occult literature; we read of seven continents, seven races, seven great orders of life, seven steps to liberation and so on. The magnetic field of the earth is nourished by the sun. The entire solar system pulsates and forces circulate, not unlike the circulation in the physical body. We are linked, through the sun, to the rest of the cosmos.

The study of correspondences reveals the great truth that all living things are part of one magnificent pattern. This is the greatest lesson we can learn from the study of astrology. With proper study, the intellect and intuition become blended in a natural, harmonious manner and man becomes a *sage*, one who sees clearly.

The ancients studied man. The human organism, so wonderfully complex, yet harmonious in all its parts became their architectural design upon which they constructed the Grand Man of the Starry Heavens. The twelve signs of the celestial zodiac were divided into sections of the human frame, so that the entire zodiacal belt was symbolized as a man bent round in the form of a circle, with the soles of his feet placed against the back of his head. Each of the twelve signs of the zodiac contains 30 degrees of space, making 360 degrees of a circle.

More depends upon the position, aspect and power of the sun and moon at birth than upon the other planets of the solar system. The sun and the moon are transmitters of stellar forces. They act as mediums and cast their gathered or reflected powers into our magnetic atmosphere, harmoniously or discordantly according to how they are aspected by the rays of the major planets.

Man has five positive points of projection and four positive centers of energy. The head, hands and feet are the five points of projection. These are symbolized by the five pointed star. The positive centers within the body are the brain, spleen, heart and generative organs. The great reception center of the body is the solar plexus. The astral system of a human body, with six (twelve by polarity) inner spinal centers, is inter-related with the physical sun and the twelve zodiacal signs. Thus is man affected by his inner and outer universe. The forces of nature, as well as the inner impulse to know Truth, works to refine and condition the body so it can be a fit instrument through which clear soul consciousness can filter and function.

COSMIC CYCLES

Science has discovered that all cells of matter, having varying periods of rhythmic motion, follow a predictable pattern beginning with their birth and controlling the process of development to maturity, even to guiding the evolutionary steps preceding the process of breaking down of, or reproducing their own species. And, it has been found that the periodicity which distinguishes the rhythm of each of these species or classifications of matter is harmoniously related to the periodicity which we can observe in the movements of the planets.

Is man a free agent or not? This is an obvious question. And, the answer is equally obvious: as long as man remains asleep to the Truth he is not free, but is subject to the forces in nature. When he awakens he learns to work harmoniously with the forces in nature and finds freedom within the framework of the whole. For a man to deny the existence of forces in his universe does not remove him from such influences. Thankfully, the workings of the forces in the universe do not depend upon man's belief or disbelief in them.

It has been observed that human life is governed, to a great degree, by forces which cause man to go through seven cycles in a year's time. This is also reflected in man's entire life span. The first seven years of earth life is the time for education and indoctrination into the culture. This is a period of self-discovery when we learn to relate to our world. From seven to fourteen years of age we notice a change in our physical characteristics as well as a rounding out of our mental nature. Then, until we reach twenty-one we develop our mental and psychic abilities, come into a sense of social responsibility and some unfoldment of intuition as well as an interest being shown in the higher things of life. For the next cycle, until the age of thirty-five, we find the most active use of mind and creative powers brought to bear on life. The next seven year cycle should see the unfoldment of an interest in the uncovering of the mysteries of life. This is a time when a person awakens from purely selfish concerns and begins to take an active interest in projects and ventures involving the welfare of others. It is at this stage that we often find a person beginning to give back to society what society gave him. The final cycle should find one turning to the contemplation of the Supreme.

To unawakened people the universal cycles, inner and outer, bring unforeseen changes in their lives. For those who are awakened they bring a welcome transformation.

Little is known of man's existence millions of years ago, or even, for that matter, a few thousand years ago. We do have similar stories and legends, however, which are to be found among all cultures and races; which point to the first beginnings. We know that from the beginning separate races evolved, each in their own time but following a similar pattern. We know that through them all the same Spirit is endeavoring to express and in the end, all men have the same destiny.

CHAPTER THREE

Ten Thousand Years of Light

Ten Thousand Years of Light

Man's history on this planet can be traced with a great degree of accuracy by a close study of the cycles through which he has moved, due to heavenly influences.

Moons revolve around their planets, and planets with their moons, revolve around the sun. The sun, takes a distant star as its central point and makes the complete orbit in about 24,000 years of earth time. This celestial phenomenon results in the backward movement of the equinoctial points around the zodiac. The sun has another motion by which it revolves around a Central Core; *the seat of power* for this solar system. This is the point in space from which Universal Magnetism acts upon life as a whole, using heavenly bodies as distribution points. The Core or center, regulates the mental forces on the inner planes. When the sun in its revolution comes to the place nearest this Center of Universal Magnetism, the mental condition of man on this planet is so refined that the soul can readily comprehend the mysteries of Spirit.

When the sun reaches the most distant place from this Center of Universal Magnetism, the mental condition of man is clouded and he cannot comprehend the finer aspects of creation or the nature of God. In the former instance we have what is termed a Golden Age and in the latter, a Dark Age. In between we have varying degrees of mass enlightenment or mass delusion, depending upon the distance of the sun from this Grand Center. Because the movement of the sun about this Center takes 24,000 years, the peak of the Golden Age and the valley of the Dark Age are 12,000 years apart.

Each of these 12,000 year periods brings a complete change in the inner nature of man, which is reflected in his world. The complete 24,000 year cycle is called an *Electric Time-Cycle*. Starting from the low point, or bottom of the Dark Age, the unfoldment of the mental condition is gradual and is divided into four noticeable stages. The time of 1,200 years, during which the sun passes through 1/20th of its orbit is called the Dark Age. In relationship to mass consciousness, the mental ability of the average person during this period is but one-fourth developed, and man cannot grasp anything but the external world. Most people at this level are materialistic because they can only comprehend that which is revealed through their five senses. The intuition, the faculty of the soul, is not yet awakened.

The second period of 2,400 years of the ascending cycle, when the sun moves through 2/20ths of its orbit, is called the Electrical Age, because during this time human intellect begins to comprehend the fine forces in nature; the electricities and their attributes which are the creating principles of the external world.

The third period of 3,600 years, during which the sun passes through 3/20ths of its orbit, is called the Mental Age, when the human intellect is able to grasp the *source* of electrical forces upon which creation depends for its existence.

The remaining fourth period during which the sun passes through 4/20ths of its orbit, is called the Golden Age or Intuitive Age, because at this level the human intellect can grasp the nature of God, that from which the material worlds have emerged. This period is 4,800 years in duration.

Reaching the peak, the descent begins, in reverse order, as the sun moves away from the Grand Center, in the same time-sequence as did the ascent. So, we see the Golden Age period is the longest of all, totaling almost 10,000 years (4,800 years ascending and 4,800 years descending). Manu, the ancient sage, wrote, "Four thousands of years, they say, is the Golden Age of the world." He referred to the very peak since several hundred years pass on either side of the uppermost part in the ascent and descent.

From 11,501 B.C., when the sun began to move away from the point of its orbit nearest the Grand Center, the intellectual powers of man on this planet began to diminish. During the 4,800 years of the descending Golden Age, the intellect, as a whole, lost the power to grasp spiritual truth. During the following 3,600 years of the descending Mental Age, the masses lost the power to grasp the subtle realms. During the 2,400 descending years of the Electrical Age, the masses lost the power to understand the nature of electricity. During the final 1,200 years of the descent, man dropped into the Dark Ages. This cosmic time table, simply and directly, explains the reason for the rise and fall of civilization.

I must explain that the rise and fall of man, in the overall sense, is not due to anything man does or does not do, but upon this electrical phenomenon by which nature is ruled. Souls incarnate during the cycles when they find an environment best suited to their karmic needs.

The period around A.D. 500 was the darkest part of the last Dark Age, and history confirms this. From that point, the sun began to move again toward the Grand Center, and the intellect of man began to be unveiled, resulting in mass awakening as the cycle moved in the direction of the Electrical Age once more. Just before A.D. 1,600, one hundred years before the onset of the present Electrical Age, a few people on the planet began to perceive the finer forces of nature. William Gilbert discovered magnetic substances. In 1609 Kepler discovered important laws of astronomy and Galileo produced the telescope. In 1621 Drebbel invented the microscope. Then, Newton became aware of the law of gravitation, and Savery made use of the steam engine. In 1720 Stephen Gray discovered the action of electricity on the human body. The new era had begun.

In the political worlds, we saw the changes that made for better government, and civilization began to advance. Through the use of the steam engine, telegraph wires,

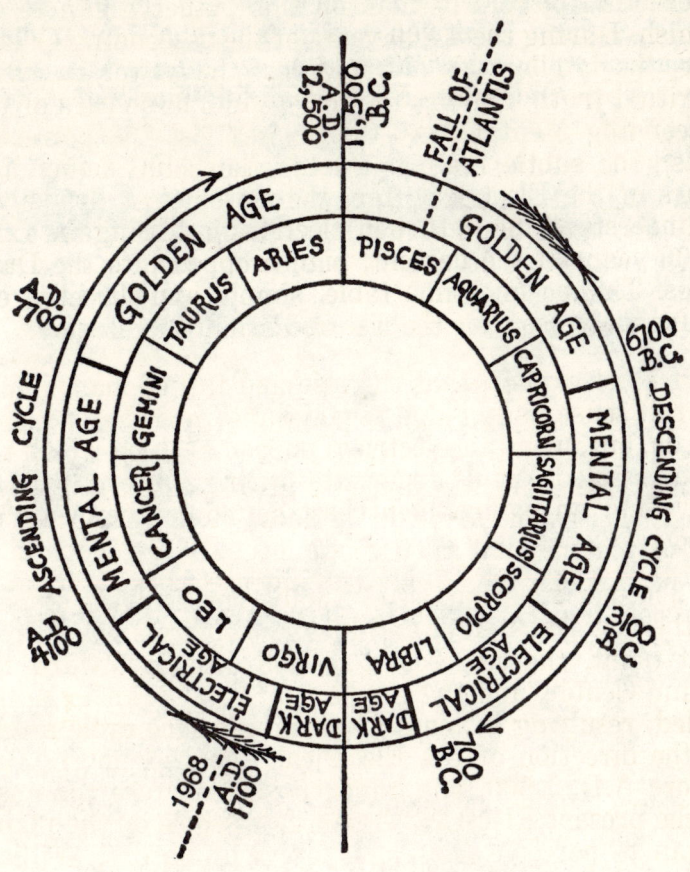

Author's note: By looking at the above diagram and starting at the top following the arrows one can trace the fall of civilization, for reasons explained in the text, as well as the current ascending cycle. As of this writing (1968) we are now 268 years into the ascending Electrical Cycle.

electric machines and other instruments of convenience the subtle matters of nature were put to practical use. Around the turn of the century, we saw the production of the airplane, improvements in radio and then, in rapid succession; television, atomic power, and great breakthroughs in understanding the building blocks of matter.

These are challenging times when man is forced to awaken to keep pace with new discoveries. Responsibility always goes hand in hand with insight. But, since this mass awakening is part of a cosmic plan, we may rest assured that the right men will always come on the scene at the right time to maintain order on this planet.

As we understand the workings of Spirit we see there is, indeed, a Creative Intelligence which is responsible for the destiny of creation. Many philosophers have blamed man for the destruction of past civilizations. Such accusations are, for the most part, misplaced, because man is but a participant and an instrument through which the Divine Intelligence works. The more God-conscious a person is, the less universal forces influence him. These forces act upon the attributes of our basic nature which make up the physical and astral bodies. When a soul is consciously in tune with the Infinite and rests in the realization of its own Self-completeness, the outer changes do not seriously affect it. This is why, during the darkest of the Dark Ages, a few God-men have been able to live ideal lives and show by example, what is possible for all men, regardless of external conditions.

Each peak of the Golden Age is higher than the one which preceded it, and the low point of each Dark Age is higher than the one which preceded it. In this way, the world, over a period of millions of years of repeating 24,000 year Electrical Time-Cycles is transformed, and quite literally, redeemed. This is the universal plan. In time, the gross worlds will be resolved into pure Spirit. "Heaven and earth will pass away, but my Word will not pass away." (Creation, subtle and gross, will be resolved but the Creative Force will remain, neutralized for a time, until, once again, creation is sent forth into expression.) At least 2,000,000,000 years remain before this solar system is dissolved. A billion is one thousand million. Minor prophets of doom to the contrary, this planet will be here for a long, long time.

For students of the occult sciences, I will mention that a mistake was made during the last Dark Age cycle in the calculations of astronomers and astrologers. Some books from India state that we are still in the Dark Age period and will remain so for another 432,000 years. This error, still widely circulated, made its appearance about 700 B.C., during the reign of Raja Parikshit. During that time, Maharaja Yudhisthira, noticing the manifestation of the coming Dark Age, turned his throne over to his grandson and retired into the seclusion of the Himalayan mountains with his wise men. There were none in the remaining court to correctly calculate the movements of the celestial bodies. The astronomers did not want to record the coming of the Dark Ages and cause fear among the people, so they recorded the beginning of the Dark Age as being the beginning of the following Electrical Age. They wanted people to believe they were riding an upward cycle instead of a downward one. However, about A.D. 499, the mistake in the almanac was noted, but not the reason for it. The almanac had recorded the length of the Dark Age as one period of 1,200 years, instead of two periods (1,200 descending and 1,200 ascending). So, the later astrologers assumed that the Dark Age years were not real years but "Years of the Gods" with one year being a day and 1,200 years amounting to 432,000 solar years. This error has now been corrected and publicized, largely through the efforts of my great guru, Swami Sri Yukteswar, who was a gifted astrologer as well as an enlightened sage. We can prove the truth of our assertions made here with our calculations as set forth and by comparing them with the outer events, as found in historical records.

Now, in this current Electrical Age, which is ascending due to the mighty pull of the Attracting Power of Spirit, the unveiling of the organs of perception is rapidly taking place and all men are coming to the realization that they are, as a whole, awakening to a new dimension in consciousness.

According to ancient prophecy, in line with our computations as set forth here and evidenced by current happenings, this is the age of space conquest. From now on, for the next 2,000 years, the strides made in this direction will be stupendous by average standards. It will not be too many years before man is able to move freely through space to the distant planets, and in times to come, other solar systems. In the ancient texts of India, we find reference to herbs, medicines, intricate surgery and humane forms of government. With the decline of civilization, for reasons explained earlier, knowledge of these things was lost. Now, as man awakens, he is beginning to once again work in harmony with nature, and will even surpass in all areas, the highest and best of the past.

ANCIENT ATLANTIS

The beginning of the descent of the last Golden Age, about 11,500 B.C. has a correlation with the legend of the fall of a once great empire known as Atlantis. This vast empire was ruled by a group of nine philosopher-kings. It had conveniences for the citizens of all classes and possessed much of the useful knowledge we have today. This large land mass was flooded as a result of cataclysmic upheavals and the destruction was total. But, before the destruction, great migrations took place, with many of the people moving from Atlantis to India, Egypt, South and North America. Plato in the *Critias* describes this Golden Age prior to the fall. It was a philosophic democracy, the arts flourished and the sciences were cultivated in great universities. Man had no enemies and war was unknown. Gradually, because of the cosmic influences, men lost their Divine Consciousness and with it, their virtues. Personal ambition and corruption ensued. Atlantis fell; and, the fortunes of men declined as civilization spiraled down through the Mental, Electrical and Dark Ages. Atlantis fell about 10,184 B.C. or approximately 1,316 years after the Golden Age began to decline.

The light that was hers lingered on because poets and philosophers preserved the story in writings and transmitted it through oral teachings. The glory of Rome was but the dying embers of a once great civilization; hence, it was doomed.

But, even during the Dark Ages, wisdom is never lost. It is carefully hidden from the eyes of the profane, veiled in symbolism and guarded by enlightened men until the time is ready for its re-emergence. Today, 268 years into the ascending Electrical Age, the time for secrecy is passing.

One-tenth of the duration of each Age is a time of mutation and over-lapping; at the end of one Age, the evidence of the Age to come begins to be apparent. And after entry into the Age, remnants of the Age just passed remain for a while. Hence, 1940 marked the point in time when we made a clean break with the last Dark Age and began an accelerated awakening.

The challenge of today is to keep pace with new discoveries. Indeed, so immense is this task that information must be stored electronically to have it available for immediate use and to conserve space. Barriers are being broken down, much to the consternation of materialistic people. Boundaries between nations are being erased as we move in the direction of world government; which must come. Prejudice, nationalism and orthodoxy is giving way to understanding, brotherhood and an universal philosophy of life.

This is part of the grand design for man; once known by the ancients, visualized by the planners of our current age and clearly realized by perceptive people.

A breaking up of the old always precedes the emergence of the new; and in this we have nothing to fear. The challenge of the next few decades is to maintain some semblance of stability while this change takes place; and we will do it.

Communications today have reduced the world's nations to a family of human beings, riding a spaceship called earth as it speeds through the ethers carrying its passengers to a most enlightened era.

CHAPTER FOUR

The Lightbearers

The Lightbearers

For millions of years the world has been blessed by the presence of enlightened God-men; men eternally aware of their divine nature. Of these God-men, the ones with the highest spiritual attainment are the *avatars*. This Sanskrit word means *descent*, and its use signifies the *descent of Divinity into flesh. An avatar is literally God appearing as man.*

The avatars bring the revealing word to man who is searching for a way out of earthy confinement. The appearance of a liberated soul serves a number of functions. Such a soul demonstrates the kind of life we all can lead. Avatars work for the good of the world and for the enlightenment of the human race. They see the involvement of the masses and know the sorrows and anxieties of the average man. But, they inwardly know their true nature as God. Because of this, they never lose themselves in the mire of human consciousness.

Every enlightened master teaches the same basic truth, the *eternal religion*. He declares himself to be "the way, the truth, and the life". Jesus said, "Believe me that I am in the Father and the Father is in me." Restating timeless truths in the language of the times, the avatar plays a role in the world, appearing as mortal man, in order to elevate mankind.

Try as we will, it is impossible for us to know God intellectually. We worship gods of our imaginings before we contemplate the Truth, because we are incapable of clearly knowing the real nature of God until our intuitive faculty is awakened. Worship of any kind, even blind devotion, is better than no worship at all, because it purifies the consciousness and awakens the sleeping soul.

Sages have classified the various distinguishable states of God-realization. Rising above this world, moving in the realization of our true nature, in tune with

Universal Will, we live by grace and are said to have attained *salvation*. In this state of conscious understanding we are *saved* from suffering due to ignorance. While we may, at this stage, still work out existing karmic patterns, we do not create any new ones. We move intuitively, following inner guidance at all times. Leaving the body in this consciousness, we do not have to return to earth against our will but we can continue our unfoldment on the more subtle astral and causal planes.

Progressing beyond the astral realms and into the awareness of the causal worlds, we become *perfected beings*, free of all subconscious ties with the astral realms and possessed of understanding of the inner nature of creation. At this stage we become true masters, able to awaken and guide others who seek the truth of life. We understand the dream of creation and how it is all held together by the will of God. Just as our dreams are maintained by our subconscious will.

Understanding the causal realms and going beyond them to the Source, a person becomes *supremely free* and no longer needs to be involved with Darkness on any level. If such a person returns to the lower causal, astral or physical realms, he is an avatar, a world savior. Limiting concepts of birth and death have no meaning to a supremely free soul. Jesus said, "If a man keep my saying he will never know death." In other words, if a person will remain in the continuous realization of Universal Consciousness, he will remain above the relativities and the considerations of beginning, ending and change.

Birth and death only have meaning in this relative world. A supremely free soul can take a body for a special purpose and can leave it at will. Again, the words of Jesus, "No man taketh it from me but I lay it down of myself. I have power to lay it down and I have power to take it up again."

Masters and avatars incarnate in man's time of need. Great souls are ever coming into the world to regenerate human consciousness. Usually, when they incarnate, there are a few years when they seek the Truth. The almost-clear memories of celestial realms from whence they have come filters through the mind and propels them onward. After awakening to the realization of their life mission, they consciously begin their ministry.

Revelation is near to every man. It is never far off. The secrets of the universe are available to all who will seek with an open heart. ("Everyone who is of Truth heareth my voice.") Some avatars appear again and again to help mankind. Buddha claimed to be the teacher of many enlightened sages in times gone by. Krishna claimed the same: "My births I know, Arjuna, thy births you remember not."

The Supreme, which controls nature, assumes any form at will for the good of creation and for the benefit of awakening souls. Avatars and masters take on bodies in order to be *lightbearers,* so that men might find freedom in God. The appearance of an avatar on the world scene is not due to the avatar's self-will, for a liberated soul only does "the will of the Father". All creation is a play of lights and shadows; it is God's drama. Some souls, upon awakening, return to complete awareness of Oneness. Others remain just this side of total Oneness, sometimes for millions of years, and take up various duties having to do with the unfoldment of mass consciousness.

Today, a number of completely self-realized men and women are on earth; some publicly, some behind the scenes, working to guide humanity through the shifting seas of life. Occasionally, an avatar will appear in public in order to make a dramatic impact on society. He is hailed as a world-teacher and establishes a new religious movement, so that men might have practical knowledge of the facts of life. Usually, an avatar remains in seclusion, guiding and assisting masters who work openly. There is but a shade of difference between an avatar and a master; merely a degree of God-perception. Ordinarily, it is the master who works with the public, awakens and trains disciples and charges them to carry on in the world, spreading the *gospel*, the good news. The advanced disciples are usually souls at the first level of mastership, ones who have attained salvation, but who have some personal karma to work out. Their selfless spiritual service under the guidance of the master is the means for their own liberation. Such disciples, among the masses who are contacted by the master, are the ones who have "ears to hear". They know the master's mission and cooperate wholeheartedly with him. In this way; God, through the avatars, masters and enlightened disciples spreads the light of Truth.

As hard as it is for some to believe, there are avatars on earth now who have retained their bodies for centuries. One of these is the avatar Babaji, who resides in the Himalayan mountains. Babaji said that he initiated Shankara, founder of the swami order in 400 A.D., as well as a number of other well known mystics, over the centuries. Some years ago, it was known that Babaji's inner circle included, among others, two American disciples.

Babaji is interested in the western world and it was he who planned that Yogananda come to America to teach yoga methods. As far as I know, there are no photographs of Babaji, because he prefers no personal publicity. He is concerned with the slow evolutionary progress of a man from century to century, and works closely with masters who are active in the world. He is not limited to the physical body which, in his case, appears ever-youthful; nor is he limited to this planet. His major work, however, has to do with the planet earth. He, along with other avatars, even while in seclusion, *sends out radiations to clear mass consciousness and subtly, but inconspicuously, influence key world figures who are receptive to telepathic impulses.*

In January 1894, Sri Yukteswar, at the request of his guru, Lahiri Mahasaya, visited a religious festival in Allahabad, India. At this time, he met Babaji who instructed him to write a book showing the underlying harmony between Christian and Hindu scriptures by giving parallel references. The book was written and published as *The Holy Science*. I too, have felt the urge to write books which set forth the eternal truths; hence, the treatise you now hold in your hands.

Babaji's chief disciple in the outer world was Lahiri Mahasaya, of Benares, India. In 1861, as a man of thirty-three years, married, with two sons; an accountant in the Military Engineering Department of the Government, Lahiri was summoned by telegram to Ranikhet, where an army post was to be established. Roaming through the nearby hills one day, thinking of the stories of saints who were said to be in that region, Lahiri came to a small clearing and there met a youthful-appearing holy man who welcomed him and told him that he, Babaji, was Lahiri's guru of incarnations past. At this meeting, the memories of his previous incarnation flooded Lahiri's mind. Shortly thereafter, he was initiated into the science of Kriya, and after several days in the highest mystical experience, was instructed to return to his home, continue his role as a householder and initiate those who would be drawn to him. He was told, furthermore, that his life was to be an example to others *that people could, even while performing their duties in society, meditate and realize God.*

Lahiri Mahasaya initiated more than five thousand people during his lifetime, before leaving his body consciously, during meditation, at age sixty-six in 1895. Before he passed, he told Sri Yukteswar that about fifty years after his passing his life story would be published and widely distributed in the west. This prophecy came to pass with the publication of Yogananda's book *Autobiography of a Yogi*, in which my guru has brilliantly set forth the stories of scores of saints.

Among Lahiri's disciples, Sri Yukteswar was the one selected to train Yogananda for the mission of introduc-

THE LIGHTBEARERS

ing the science of self-realization to the west. Yukteswar was a married man, with a daughter, when he met Lahiri Mahasaya. It was after his wife died, and his daughter was grown, that he became a swami. Sri Yukteswar, whose monastic name means "union with God as Light" was a brilliant man; widely read and highly illumined. He had two ashrams, one at Puri and another in Calcutta, where he trained disciples who came to him. He left his body in 1936, at the age of eighty. He too passed consciously, by an act of will, when his time came.

All of these masters came with a specific mission; to re-introduce to an awakening world, the scientific way to God-realization.

A master leaves writings and trained disciples so that his ministry extends through time. Our intense yearning for God-realization causes us to be put in tune and in contact with, either a master who is embodied, or one of his disciples through whom the power of Spirit flows. Masters advise against the effort to contact "invisible masters" in meditation or in a seance room. It is far better to receive oral instruction from the lips of an embodied master, or his representative, than to try to make mental contact for the purpose of practical instruction. A person who is new on the path is not sufficiently awakened to receive clear instruction from discarnate masters; and what goes on in seance rooms where masters are purported to manifest is, for the most part, a mockery.

In the ancient writings, it is recorded that the Buddha told his disciples, "Know that from time to time a free soul is born into the world, a fully enlightened one, blessed and worthy, abounding in wisdom and goodness, happy with the knowledge of the worlds, unsurpassed as a guide to erring mortals, a teacher of gods and men. He proclaims the truth both in its letter and in its spirit, lovely in its origin, lovely in its progress, lovely in its consummation. A higher life doth he make known in all its purity and all its perfectness."

Transcending any permanent identification with mortality, the avatars belong to a different race. The Buddha, after his enlightenment, returned home to visit his father, wearing simple clothing. His father was perplexed at the sight of him and asked, "Why is this?" Buddha gently replied, "My father, such is the custom of my race." His parent asked, "What race?" To which the Buddha stated, "The Buddhas who have been and who shall be; Of these I am and what they did I do."

The story follows the general pattern of all enlightened souls. In early manhood he went into seclusion to seek the answers to life. Following the advice of other ascetics he tried self-mortification, fasting, sleeplessness and long hours of intense concentration. Still, the vision of Truth did not come to him. Then, he contemplated the nature of life, vowing never to move until he attained wisdom. "What is the source of human misery and sorrow", he inquired within; "Why old age, disease and death?" And, as he contemplated, firm in his resolve, the revelations came.

Suddenly the vision of the successions of many births and deaths in the stream of life was revealed to him. He saw birth frustrated by the threat of death, he saw joy balanced by grief, desire by discontent. He saw how man lives a victim of his karma or his subconscious conditionings. He saw that this went on, seemingly without end. He asked, "Why does this not stop?" Then, he saw; it was karma which drove man onwards, in spite of himself. He reasoned further, if a man could anchor his attention in the Infinite, the Permanently Real, instead of to passing things, he might eventually transcend things and win peace. So, enlightenment came to him as his awareness soared beyond the reflection-worlds, the realms of lights and shadows; and he saw the cause of it all. Thus it was that he experienced the realization of the Supreme Self.

Buddha began to teach. Instead of saying that God spoke through him, he only claimed enlightenment. He had seen the way and he wanted to point others to it. He was extremely patient and considerate of the shortcomings of the average man. Like Jesus, he taught the return of good for evil, love for hate; and remained silent when abused and misunderstood. He walked from town to town and talked to those who were drawn to him.

His favorite teaching was the *Four Noble Truths*, in which he taught that life is pain, pain is due to selfish desire, and the way to end pain is to put an end to selfish desire and unreasoned cravings. His emphasis was upon right conduct, not upon empty ritual, worship or abstract metaphysical discussion. He refused to be drawn into endless controversies as to whether the world had a beginning and end, or whether there was purpose to the cosmic drama. He termed such activities as the entanglement of intellectual speculation, leading nowhere. He never taught that God could be known, but did stress that Truth could be experienced. Like Jesus, he knew that the realization of Truth alone would make men free.

Buddha's final lesson was this: To his disciple, Ananda, he said, "And whosoever, either now or after I am gone, shall be a lamp unto themselves, and a refuge unto themselves, shall betake themselves to no external refuge, but, holding fast to the Truth as their lamp . . . shall not look for refuge to any one besides themselves; it is they who shall reach the topmost height. But, they must be anxious to learn." His last words, we are told, were, "Subject to decay are compound things. Strive with earnestness." He passed from this world about 483 B.C., at the age of eighty.

Jesus, according to tradition, came on the scene about five hundred years after Buddha, during the middle of the last descending Dark Age period. He, too, was misunderstood by his contemporaries, and is still misunderstood by millions in today's world. Jesus never expected a world-shaking transformation which would result in the establishing of the kingdom of heaven on earth in his lifetime. What he said was, "There are some standing here who will not taste of death until they see the kingdom come with power." But, he was speaking of souls who were ripe for spiritual awakening who would literally inherit the kingdom of fulfillment even while embodied. He clearly stated, "My kingdom is not of this world."

In the latter part of the last century, a simple illiterate man, Sri Ramakrishna, was hailed by scholars and religious leaders alike, as an incarnation of God. A careful study of his life leaves no doubt that he was truly a great soul who had come to earth to assist in the regeneration of mankind. He once confided to some close disciples that before he incarnated he knew he would need helpers on earth, so he sought them out. On a high astral plane, he saw a man absorbed in profound meditation and asked the man to follow him to earth to assist him with his mission. The meditating sage agreed. Years later, when Ramakrishna was enlightened, a young man was brought to him by a disciple. Instantly, Ramakrishna recognized him as that same sage with whom he had communed before incarnating. The young man became a disciple and entered monastic life as Swami Vivekananda; later he came to America to found many of the Vedanta Centers in key cities.

Great masters, while outwardly playing different roles in order to serve the greatest number of people, inwardly recognize each other and fully approve of various ministries. Yogananda used to say, "The masters rejoice in each others company; only their disciples argue."

The avatars and masters, fully aware of their divine nature and functioning as they are impelled by the Supreme Will, are a band of enlightened saviors; *a brotherhood of Light*. But, this brotherhood which is the true one, has nothing to do with the outer organizations which have tried to fashion themselves after that which is real. *Entry into this true brotherhood is effected as a result of the initiate's God-consciousness and the degrees passed through are the different levels of realization.*

One might ask the question, "If the masters are so enlightened and have such great ability, why do they not come on the world scene with a greater flourish and wipe out war, poverty and all of man's inhumanity to man?" The answer is this; they can only inspire and instruct, they cannot rule by force. Also, we might say, "the play must go on."

As part of the overall plan of world enlightenment, from time to time, spiritual teachers with different levels of understanding come forth. It is interesting to note that in the eighteen-sixties, about one hundred years ago, while Babaji was charging Lahiri Mahasaya with the responsibility of taking the lost art of deep meditation to the world, in this country a spiritual revival was beginning. Christian Science was born; and a host of independent truth teachers drew the attention of the public. The so-called *New Thought* movement began to evolve and today has grown to impressive proportions; even though the general teachings offered by the member groups only go so far in the explanation of things. New Thought meets a need for hundreds of thousands of people who seek a better way of life, but are not yet ready for complete self-realization.

Near the turn of the century, Charles Fillmore, who thought of himself as a reincarnated Indian yogi, with his wife, Myrtle, started the Unity School of Practical Christianity which, today, has spread to the ends of the earth. A decade later, Ernest Holmes began to teach, and his ministry has blossomed into the influential Religious Science movement, teaching the *Science of Mind* through lectures by ministers in scores of churches, classes, books and magazines. Under his given name, and his pen-name, *Yogi Ramacharaka*, William Walker Atkinson, wrote dozens of books on eastern philosophy slanted to western man, as well as tomes on mental magic, positive thinking and mind power. Ernest Holmes, Ernest Wilson (who was later to join Unity) Paramahansa Yogananda, Emmet Fox and others taught how-to-live classes to thousands of people in huge auditoriums around the country. Norman Vincent Peale, inspired by Unity and Science of Mind, has reached millions through the printed word, lectures, radio and television. Until recently, Joel S. Goldsmith, surely one of the great teachers of our time, carried his message of the *Infinite Way* to the major cities of the world.

Around the globe, we see Spirit awakening in man: In Japan, Dr. Masaharu Taniguchi heads a ten million member truth movement, Seicho-No-Ie, with branches all over the world; the School of Truth, with headquarters in South Africa, sends millions of pieces of literature free of charge to interested seekers; colleges and universities are hot-beds of interest in meditation and psychical research.

It is well established that the god of human imagining is dead; no longer applicable to the needs of modern man. The established church is undergoing a renovation from within. Spirit is moving through the hearts of men, speeding the awakening and bringing greater understanding, which is being reflected in improved social conditions and a better way of life for the citizens of the world.

The fundamentalists are right, the world is coming to an end; the world which has been known for so long. We are awakening to a new day and a new social order; thanks to the Lightbearers and sincere truth teachers who have unselfishly served in their appointed places.

CHAPTER FIVE

The Glorious Destiny

The Glorious Destiny

There is a way to insure steady unfoldment on the spiritual path and it has been described in the great scriptures of the world by fully illumined sages who, themselves, have realized the Ultimate Good. Any sincere person who will abide by the suggestions set forth will learn to be in tune with life and experience the utmost happiness and inner peace.

Traditionally, before a student is accepted for initiation, he has to prepare himself through a program of self-discipline. This is not merely a testing of the candidate's sincerity, it is necessary for his mental, emotional and spiritual welfare. Before being introduced to the inner mysteries, it is important that we learn to live in a balanced, orderly and responsible manner. And it is likewise important that our motives be pure.

There is only one way to God-realization. Systems, methods and techniques differ, but the way remains the same for all of us. When we begin to perceive the true way we find a transformation taking place within us. We begin to desire the company of wise and enlightened teachers. All men ask sooner or later, "What must I do to be saved?" Of course, a person who is floundering in Darkness is in need of being saved; from the pain and troubles of mortal existence. The answer is always the same, "Leave the world, with its vain imaginings and false hopes and follow Me; follow the leading of Spirit."

But, how many are willing to go all the way? How many are, instead, content to dabble at the fringes of the Ocean of Truth? This is the problem; the majority in this world do not want to be enlightened because they "love darkness more than light". Krishna, in the Bhagavad Gita stated it was way, "Out of a thousand, one seeks me. Out of a thousand who thus seek, one knows me as I really am." Too many truth students are not really serious about self-realization; they seek a little understanding so they can be more efficient in their selfish, misguided personal ventures. And, this is why so many fail on the spiritual path. They forget the great promise, "Seek ye first the kingdom of heaven and its righteousness and all things will be added unto you." The testimony of the masters is that all who are in tune with God are automatically provided for and live trouble-free lives.

We have the responsibility of preparing ourselves for enlightenment. As the wind currents move the clouds and the sun is revealed, *so our discipline clears away the clouds of error and false thinking and the glory of the soul is revealed.* Seven things are required of us as we prepare for initiation.

1. *Proper Education* —We must see to it that we are properly informed concerning the facts of life. We must know, at least intellectually; what God is, the origin and nature of the soul, and the cause and destiny of creation. This information is set forth in this book.

2. *We Must Go All The Way* — We must decide to finish what we set out to do; we must go all the way on the spiritual path. Too often we waver in our intention and try new theories when a few more steps on the path would have resulted in enlightenment. Even if we go through life without noticeable results, if at the last moment we break through and perceive Reality, we will be liberated. A firm decision in the beginning will organize our thoughts and feelings, on all levels, and supply us with the motive force to be steady on the path.

3. *We Must Recognize our Debt to Society* — We are to fulfill our duties in this world in the right Spirit. The race which produced us must be upheld and society must be maintained on a stable level. It is our duty to serve others as we have been served by those who preceded us. If we fail to recognize our

obligation to society, we are not fit for self-realization.

4. *Responsibility Must be in Proportion to Understanding*—We are wise and responsible if we work for the good of our fellow man according to the talents and abilities we possess. To do less is to shirk our responsibility and to try to do more is to play a false role in life. It does not really matter what we do in this world as long as we perform some worthwhile service, because all work is necessary. We are to work with the attitude that the Infinite is working through us. We are to let the service we render be the reward, and not look for appreciation or recognition. If we do the best we can to fulfill our own destiny, it will lead us to self-realization eventually, even if we fail to perform perfectly. But, if we try to live out a role which is not ours, if we try to pattern ourselves after another person, whose destiny may differ from ours, we not only experience eventual frustration as a result of being out of tune with life but we fail to unfold according to our own inner pattern.

To conform for the sake of convenience is to stifle initiative and growth. To work for the effects of actions, for the praise of others, or to compensate for personal inadequacies, is to live on the surface of life and be disillusioned.

5. *Our Motives Must be Pure* — We should seek self-realization for the sake of enlightenment alone and not for any personal gains which might manifest along the way. If we desire only to know the truth about life, we will learn to see, as Sons of God, we need nothing, for "all that the Father has is ours".

6. *We Must Not Become Diverted from the Goal* — Whatever psychic experiences we have, as attrac-

tive as they may be, must not cause us to stray from the ultimate goal. Any spontaneous happening, if not sought, can be accepted as part of our total experience, of course. But fascination with psychic phenomena is just as much a barrier to self-realization as over-concern with the things of this physical world.

People who, through the use of drugs, self-hypnosis, concentration on wrong goals, or mental aberrations, succeed in catching a glimpse of the inner realms are not necessarily enlightened as a result. A true mystic is one who is awake on all levels and who clearly discerns the Source of all manifestation and knows that outer appearances, including the astral and mental realms, are but reflections of the Real. He is therefore able to move through the world intelligently as a knower of Truth and is never deluded. Free of ego and ignorance he desires nothing except to be an instrument through and as which the Infinite fulfills Its purpose; the awakening and enlightenment of all souls.

7. *We Must Maintain the Right Attitude* — To maintain the right attitude at all times requires self-discipline and constant remembrance of who we are. We are to always see others as we see ourselves; as God expressing. Therefore, every person we meet is deserving of our respect. Our attitude should, at all times, indicate that we are relying upon the Infinite and never, even for a moment, that we are relying upon a person, an organization or outer situation for security. Of course, we are to work with people and with responsible organizations which have been created for the welfare of society, but always with the understanding that God is expressing through all outer appearances. When we have become firmly grounded and are ready for spiritual wakening, conditions will be adjusted so that we are drawn into contact with a true guru who is God's representative on earth and

who can help us pierce the veil which has kept us from the vision of Truth.

THE GURU-DISCIPLE RELATIONSHIP

There are thousands of teachers in the world but few gurus. A teacher, according to his understanding, teaches the laws of life. But, many teachers are only dimly aware of their own divine nature and spend their time teaching about the outer worlds; physical, astral and mental. This is their function. They show people how to get along in the outer worlds and prepare them for the coming of the guru; the one who awakens and reveals the glories of the soul.

One may have many teachers but the guru-disciple bond is eternal. The relationship of guru to disciple is not to be taken lightly. In effect, the guru assumes responsibility for the disciple through incarnations until the disciple is fully illumined. The disciple's responsibility is to pay reverent attention to the guru's instructions and try to follow them, for his own welfare. The guru is self-realized and therefore wants nothing from the disciple. He desires only to serve as God's instrument in order to awaken souls and show them the way to everlasting life.

There are of course, teachers who cast themselves in the role of a guru before they are self-realized and they lead students astray. And, there are disciples who come to a true guru, but are not ready to surrender self-will and follow the advice which is given for their own spiritual progress. In either instance, favorable results are not forthcoming. But, a guru, anchored in timelessness, has infinite patience. He cannot force a disciple to do anything; he can only awaken, inspire and provide true instruction.

From the moment a person is accepted by his guru, part of his karmic load is lifted. He ceases to become more involved with useless projects and his attention is directed to the goal of life. Because of the disciple's at-

THE GLORIOUS DESTINY

tunement with the guru, he finds that his consciousness begins to clear. The God-consciousness of the guru elevates the disciple, dispels his doubts and awakens subtle currents on deeper levels. I noticed this almost immediately after I had met Paramahansa Yogananda. Not only was my spiritual resolve strengthened, but I found concentration easier and a sense of *aliveness* pervaded my entire being. Truly has the ancient sage declared, "To be in tune with the guru is to be in tune with God."

A guru always suggests, "Try what I ask and see the results for yourself." This, after all, is the test; does reverent adherence to the guru's counsel result in greater self-realization? If we are in tune, it always does.

Through the guru, and the line from which he is descended, there flows wave after wave of power and grace. Enlightened people know this. All gurus who play an outward role in the world can trace their spiritual lineage through a succession of enlightened teachers all the way back to the Source. Of course, each one of us is God expressing, but as long as we are involved with creation, we are wise to recognize the definite flow of Life and Light which passes to us through an unbroken line of illumined gurus. This is why you will always see a guru pay his respects to his own guru. He knows there is a channel through which power flows into this world. To be disrespectful of one's guru is a sign of ignorance.

Most gurus, because they are embodied, have taken on some sense of delusion in order to function here. While they may have subconscious conditionings and personal desires, they are always inwardly aware of their divine mission and, shortly before they leave the world, they meditate and cleanse themselves of anything which might tend to hold them back. Some enlightened teachers decide, before incarnating, to temporarily forget the total Truth in order to enter this dimension. When their work is finished, they awaken completely, pass over the responsibility of their mission to chosen disciples and consciously leave the body. They then continue their duties on the astral or causal levels.

My guru, Yogananda, after his passing, continued his work on the high astral planes; even as his guru, Sri Yukteswar, when he passed, went to a refined astral planet to act as a savior of souls making their transition from the astral to the causal cosmos. But, before he left, Yogananda trained many disciples to carry on his work.

I was accepted as a disciple by Yogananda early in 1950 and received Kriya initiation from him personally later that year. He ordained me in November 1951 and authorized me to carry on in his spirit; which I have tried to do ever since.

In truth, God is the only guru; but God appears on the earthly scene as the personal guru so that seeking souls might have a point of contact with the Infinite. Without this personal contact, people would wander endlessly in delusion, not knowing the way out.

I am often asked, "Where can I find a guru?" And, hard as it is to say, I must answer, "When you are ready; spiritually ripened, God as the guru will come into your life." While I know that hundreds of thousands will find inner peace through the line of gurus I represent, I also know that my gurus are not the only line and that there are other enlightened ones working for the good of man. We are drawn to the spiritual link with which we have an affinity, and often, with which we have worked before in other incarnations. While all gurus teach essentially the same message, the wave-length is different; which is why some people are drawn to certain gurus and others to different ones.

Some will say, "I don't need a guru, I can find God on my own!" But, observe their lives; see their confusion, their misdirected activities, their discontent. To yearn for realization and to work with an enlightened guru is wisdom and the quickest way to liberation.

TRUE INITIATION

Initiation is an entry to a larger life. Of course, every time we have a breakthrough in consciousness we are, to some degree, initiated. But, here I am referring to true spiritual initiation, which opens the door to the inner realms. When the candidate for initiation has prepared himself, and has met his guru, he is ready for true initiation.

Two things happen at initiation; definite instruction is given to the disciple, along with a technique for meditation and, if conditions are right, the disciple is spiritually awakened. To awaken a person without giving instruction in meditation is not wise because it opens the doors between layers of consciousness and the disciple has no way of controlling his thoughts and emotions. To impart instruction without awakening is not effective because the initiate will then work mechanically with his technique but will not gain results or spiritual insight.

This is why, even though I have explained meditation techniques in my books, I reserve the personal responsibility for initiating students into Kriya. The practice of Kriya, without a full personal explanation and the initiation ceremony, will not be effective. I do not say this in order to control the behavior of truth seekers or to dominate their lives, for I have no wish to do this. I say this because it is true.

Before an initiation ceremony, the guru prepares himself by meditating, becoming attuned to his own line of gurus and by becoming fully God-conscious. The disciple should prepare himself by meditating in order to be receptive. At initiation the guru meditates with the disciple and transfers his consciousness to the disciple; arousing latent forces and awakening the intuition. He actually casts his spiritual mantle over the disciple and the disciple receives as much as he is ready to receive at the moment. Even if the disciple does not feel any inner awakening at the time, the work has been done and a permanent bond has been established. As the disciple meditates and remains in tune with the Infinite, the inner activity increases and the rapport between him and his guru (and the guru's line of enlightened masters) becomes more evident.

No hypnosis is involved, and no attempt made by the guru to bring the disciple under his personal influence for selfish purposes. This is a very real happening and is for the good of the new initiate. Everything in creation is built up of layers of consciousness and at the core of everything is pure Being. During initiation, pure Being in the disciple is quickened and begins to work its way to the surface, transforming the nature of the disciple in the process.

Now, after initiation, the disciple's responsibility is to *practice meditation and try always to be inwardly aware of his nature as Spirit*. If he has any questions he can find the answers in the scriptures or the writings of his guru. Or, if the guru is accessible, he can ask him directly. Even without the availability of scriptures or the guru, an initiate can meditate, clear his mind, relax in the awareness of his real nature and guidance will come forth. No longer is the initiate on the outside of things; now he is consciously on the spiritual path and his liberation is assured.

The new initiate should not be upset if dramatic changes do not immediately occur in his life; if habits are not easily overcome or if he lapses in his spiritual practice. We have been dreaming the mortal dream for incarnations and we should not suppose that the touch of the master will, in a moment, banish the darkness. At least we are on the way, we have made a definite step in the right direction and we have the assurance of eventual freedom if we persist.

More and more, as we meditate and try to remain in tune with God, we find a subtle change taking place. The inner Light becomes more apparent and filters through us with ever increasing force.

While we should try to eradicate negative tendencies and habits which are not suitable for physical, mental and emotional health, we should not become despondent or think ourselves to be unspiritual if some habits and urges cling to us. We should continue our spiritual practices in the conviction that, in time, all will be made right. There are many people, who live on the surface of life, who are smug in their belief that their extreme self-discipline and self-denial is somehow a mark of spiritual attainment when, in fact, they are merely egotistical and vain; almost totally devoid of true understanding.

As we meditate and practice to the best of our ability we find that the *negation of our lower nature is blended with the uplift of Spirit, and this synchronization brings about the purification and transformation of human consciousness*. The great master Babaji, who is the first in my line of gurus, used to quote the Bhagavad Gita when initiating disciples: "Even a little practice of true meditation awakens man to the realization of his true nature and banishes ignorance, which is the basis of fear and distress."

As far as our conduct is concerned, we should see to it that our environment is harmonious, that we are well fed, obtain sufficient rest and exercise, and that all of our activities are regulated by reason. When the disciplined mind is established in God, all desires will be harmonized. Regulation of all desires, rather than denial, is true self-control. We do not have to deaden the senses and deny the heart to be spiritual. The three things which are advised are; regulation of desire, recognition that God is appearing as all things and all happenings and obedience to the laws of life which allows for supreme happiness and spiritual attainment. This is the way of an initiate.

CHAPTER SIX

Steps to Mystical Experience

Steps to Mystical Experience

The complete explanation of mind control and the art of meditation is to be found in my book *This is Reality* so I will not duplicate the instruction in this chapter, except to mention the eight steps to mystical experience.

These eight steps are; *ethical conduct, observance of spiritual principles, proper meditation posture, reversal of the flow of life force and attention, the interiorization of attention, concentration, meditation and the realization of Oneness.*

When a person feels the pull of the Magnetic Attraction and yearns to know the Ultimate Truth, his attention is turned within to the *third eye* center, the point from which the life forces flow into the body and from there, out through the senses into contact with the physical realms. By correctly turning the attention within, we are able to withdraw from the outer worlds for a while and rise above all identification with it.

In the beginning, this may require effort, even if we are firmly resolved in our practice, because we have been accustomed to letting the attention flow in an outward direction. But, with practice we can successfully turn within and find the fulfillment we sought so long in mundane realms. Man, with his attention flowing outward tends to think solely in terms of outer goals. Since change is certain in this world, no outer attainment is permanent. Therefore, one who is totally outwardly directed is doomed to eternal disappointment. On the other hand, one who learns to reside within, in the realization of his true nature, is able to function in this world freely, with understanding. As we daily withdraw from the world, we are gradually freed from the chain of cause and effect.

In deep meditation we neutralize the flows of vital force in the body and bring ourselves under control. As

STEPS TO MYSTICAL EXPERIENCE

we quiet the action of the heart and lungs, we enter into total relaxation, which is more satisfying than sleep. In the Bhagavad Gita, we read, "That meditation expert becomes eternally free who, seeking the Supreme Goal, is able to withdraw from external phenomena by fixing his concentration at the third eye center and by neutralizing the flow of vital forces in the body; and to control his mind and intellect; and to banish desire, fear and anger."

Steady meditation soon brings the initiate into an emerging awareness of the inner realms. Transcending for a time the awareness of the outer world, the meditation expert becomes free from sensory delusions, the realm of Darkness.

Breathing, the flow of vital forces and the activity of the mind are interconnected. By centering the attention at the third eye, we are able to still the mind, neutralize the flow of vital forces in the body and calm the breath. Over a period of time, a subtle transformation takes place from within; the causal and astral vehicles become enlivened and this results in physical well being, though this is not the goal of meditation.

In deep meditation we release ourselves from bodily identification and merge with the healing currents of the cosmos. In this way, we are recharged with pure Light.

This meditation method is scientific because it enables us to disconnect the mind from the things of the world. In this way, we are able to gain access to pure knowledge and return to awareness of the world with understanding. Thus, we are able to live fully in this world from our true Center, instead of being at the mercy of subconscious urgings and fleeting promises which are offered to us on all sides. The proper practice of meditation literally quickens our spiritual progress as we condense experience through concentration.

Nothing will bring the satisfaction and realization that comes as a result of proper meditation and living the true spiritual life. Intellectual knowledge alone will never satisfy us; nor will it stand by us in our moments of need. Buddha said, "Only he who lives the life will know the doctrine." Only the person who really lives from the inmost core of his being will know the truth about life; not as others think it is, but as it really is.

Meditation is not difficult. All that is required is a desire to practice and the discipline to take the time to do it. We are not to meditate for any purpose other than self-realization. True, greater realization will result in peace of mind. But, if we seek these things for themselves, instead of seeking enlightenment, we meditate for the wrong reasons. If we have personal problems they can be solved as we clear the mind and live in harmony with the basic laws of life. I repeat, meditation is for the purpose of experiencing self-realization.

HOW TO PRACTICE MEDITATION

In a quiet place, where you will not be disturbed, sit in a comfortable chair, with the spine straight and the body relaxed. Direct your attention to the point between the eyebrows and *look and listen within with an attitude of expectancy*. Do not try to make anything happen nor visualize anything specific. Any attempt to visualize or make something happen will be mental effort; we must transcend the mind so that intuition will awaken. Awakened intuition will reveal everything.

While meditating you might perceive inner *light, the cosmic sound, a sense of joy, bliss, peace, love, omnipresence, omniscience or omnipotence*. These are *attributes* of God but should only be perceived as points of contact with the Infinite and not as ends in themselves. For instance, it is possible to become rapt in light and joy and find happiness in the good feeling without ever going beyond this stage to enlightenment. So, whatever you perceive, however it happens, accept it and try to go beyond it; knowing that what you seek is beyond all form and manifestation. Pure Being is that which is at the core of all outer expressions.

If the mind wanders at first, keep the attention focused at the third eye and become aware of the movement of your breath. This will calm the mind and withdraw your attention from surrounding distractions. It will also keep you aware in the moment, so you will not think of the past, present or future. When you are inwardly calm, become *anchored* at the third eye, trying to *pierce the veil with your intuition*. Eventually, you will rest in the awareness of Being - Existence.

Remain in this awareness for as long as you can. Before long, the pull of the subconscious will cause you to once again identify with your body and mental impressions. But, at least you have made a breakthrough. With repeated practice you will be able to remain in pure meditation for longer and longer periods of time. And you will find that your inner awareness is present even when you are actively involved with your daily duties. You will function in this world in a responsible manner but with a sense of inner detachment, as one in a conscious dream. While working within the framework of time and space, you will know that you are timeless and beyond all relative appearances. This is *continuous God-consciousness. Continuous God-consciousness is the goal of human existence.* When we are able to function in the world and never forget our divine nature, we are free.

Proper meditation releases heretofore repressed energies which begin to circulate through the nervous system. This is why people who meditate have an inner radiance; their eyes are luminous, their magnetism obvious.

Even during the hours of sleep a God-conscious person is aware. His dreams are celestial and he often comes to the surface after a period of sleep and easily enters into meditation. I know a man who, after thirty years of meditation practice, is able to bypass the subconscious entirely. He meditates at night and when he retires, continues to meditate. Entering the Light, he remains until morning, merged in God. When we function from the superconscious level of mind instead of the subconscious, we are inwardly aware even though the body outwardly exhibits the characteristics of sleep. A fully self-realized person is always inwardly the same even though he seems to be asleep, awake or in deep meditation. The awareness of Being is never dimished.

In ordinary instances meditation should be practiced twice a day. Twenty minutes to a half hour is suitable to start, because regular short meditation periods keep the inner current flowing and is better than longer, less frequent sessions. Of course, if you have the time and the inclination, you can meditate for a longer period with benefit. Or you can meditate with a group of people who are serious on the path.

We should be careful that we do not use meditation as an excuse to become introverted and withdraw from our responsibilities. Remember, we have a two-fold responsibility; to *meditate and experience self-realization* and to *perform a useful service to society* as long as we are here. In fact, the performance of useful service, offering it to the Infinite, frees us from karmic involvement and makes meditation that much easier.

Some people, because of their outgoing nature, find it difficult to meditate for a long period of time. They can perform useful work in this world with a sense of detachment and find freedom. While we meditate and work, if we have a yearning to know the Truth, we will be propelled in the right direction. In time, this yearning to know is transformed into an awareness that God is expressing through us and in this way we are liberated.

STEPS TO MYSTICAL EXPERIENCE

Proper meditation, like the study of scriptures and truth books, awakens dormant memories of our soul nature. It also awakens past mental impressions of experiences realized in previous incarnations. The point is not to try to recall past embodiments, of course, but to recall our original condition, as Jesus prayed, "Father, glorify thou me, with thine own self, with the glory that was mine before the world was." This is the highest yearning of the soul; to consciously remember how it was in the beginning, before creation was outpictured on the screen of time and space.

There exists today, some confusion and even competition, between such ways as zen, yoga, Christian mysticism and other systems. There is no reason for confusion or for a playing up of differences because all mystical teachings are, at the core, the same. For instance, *zen* is an abbreviation of the word *za-zen*, which is a Japanese version of *chan*, which is the Chinese word for the Sanskrit *dhyana*, or *contemplation*. Zen is derived from the teachings of the Buddha, who was an Indian saint. Zen *satori* is the same as yoga samadhi, which is the same as the Christian mystic's *illumination*. St. Anthony, St. Theresa and a host of other Christian saints wrote of their inner experiences which parallel the experiences of the mystics of the ages.

Literally, "Truth is one, men call it by various names." Presented in these pages is the eternal religion, the way to self-realization which changes not. Garbed in myriad disguises, clouded by scriptural symbolism, the way has always been set forth and has been discerned by men of intuitive vision.

I first learned of meditation from books on yoga which I read during my high school years. But, no success came until I met my guru and began to practice according to his explicit instructions; which I offer you here. And, over the years I have noticed something quite revealing; all whom I have known who have gotten good results in meditation are individuals who *felt worthy* of good results. In our spiritual practice, as in any other venture, our attitude is important. If we feel worthy of success, if we have the right "self-image", we will be successful.

I have learned that proper identification is important. How many times have we repeated, "We become like the people with whom we associate, either physically or mentally!" And, it is true. By associating with the average man who is lost in self-condemnation, and confused by conflicting urges, we despair. But, by associating with God-like people, we soon become God-like.

This is why I urge you to read about enlightened people and why I write as much as I do. I know there is need for inspiration and proper direction in life. We all have what it takes to make the grade on the spiritual path, but we require constant inspiration and motivation.

During meditation we are becoming aware of God, our real nature. And, as we continue we become enlightened. As rays of God, we have become involved and lost our way. This is only a temporary situation. Because we are rays of God, we will awaken and divest ourselves of everything that distorts our vision and understanding; and this is what the spiritual life is all about.

In truth, if we could but relax the conscious mind and give up our vain imaginings and false notions and just rest in self-awareness; only God would exist. This is the key to successful meditation; *to erase the ego, let go of all preconceived ideas and opinions and just Be.*

Some critics of meditation exclaim that it is the way of the other-worldly; those who would retreat from life. You know this is not the truth at all. We only withdraw for a time in order to become self-complete so that we can enter into total involvement with life in an intelligent and responsible manner.

In the deepest meditation we pass over the boundaries which divide the different layers of consciousness and become aware of That which is the True Existence. Then, in thoughtless, breathless adoration we realize the Eternal. If we had words we might pray, as did the writer of this ancient Sanskrit hymn, "*I salute the supreme teacher, the Truth, whose nature is bliss, who is the giver of the highest happiness, who is pure wisdom, who is beyond all dualities and infinite like the sky, who is beyond words, who is one and eternal, pure and still, who is beyond all change and phenomena, and who is the silent witness to all our thoughts and emotions—I salute Truth, the supreme teacher.*"

CHAPTER SEVEN

Seven Levels of Soul Unfoldment

Seven Levels of Soul Unfoldment

Awakening to the full realization of our soul nature, we pass through seven distinct levels or stages of awareness; corresponding to the seven levels through which Spirit passed during the descent into gross form. In other words, as we awaken, we retrace our steps until we become fully aware of the Source, as it was before creation appeared. Becoming progressively self-realized, we experience revelation after revelation.

From material creation to pure Spirit the stages are: gross creation, perceived through the five senses; fine electrical matters, the astral realms; the stage of magnetic poles and aura-electricities; the causal realms; the *door* to the inner kingdom, polarized ray of Spirit or soul consciousness; the Perfect World, the sphere of spiritual reflection; the realm of Universal Intelligence; and finally, the realm of God, the Eternal Reality. The first three planes comprise material creation and the last three comprise the spiritual realms, the counterpart of the appearance-worlds. The fourth level is the connecting link or *door* between the inner and outer realms.

These seven recognizable changes are apparent to us as follows:

1. *Gross Consciousness* — At this stage a person is fully involved with the physical world because he is sense-bound and cannot perceive anything beyond it.

2. *Astral Consciousness* — At this stage a person is somewhat awakened and begins to show an interest in things of a psychic nature. He becomes aware of the existence of finer forces in his own body and in all of nature, although he does not understand their workings. At this level he may begin to study in order to understand this subtle realm of which he has become aware.

3. *Causal Consciousness*—At this level a person awakens and begins to understand the subtle mental causes for creation, becomes proficient in the use of mind-science and learns to control outer effects by first regulating inner causes.

4. *The Door to the Inner Realms* — At this level, one feels a strong urge to retire within; and learning to meditate, contemplates the Infinite. Here, he contemplates his true nature, as a soul, as being separate from the mind and other encasements. Thus, he embarks on the true spiritual path which leads to total liberation. Before this, at the three lower levels, his attention was turned outward and he was aware of the existence of the different levels but not the source of them. At this fourth stage, the spiritual aspirant removes the sense of ego, rises above the mind, and feeling nature and uses the intellect, illumined by intuition, to discern the difference between the Real and the reflections which appear as creation. This results in his understanding the true nature of Darkness, the fabric of nature, and in this way he attains release from bondage and becomes a free soul.

5. *The Realm of Completeness*—Having seen through the four components making up the Darkness, the soul is free of involvement with the worlds and functions in realms of light. This is heaven, the World of Reality, where perfected beings; Sons of God dwell.

6. *Realm of Universal Intelligence*—Here we find the supremely free souls who "sit at the right hand of the Father". These souls are aware of their individuality and of the ocean of Spirit at the same time. Their realization is incomprehensible to the average person. Many such souls remain for millions of years in this realm. Sometimes they voluntarily descend into the causal, astral and physical realms

and are the avatars and saviors of mankind. They inwardly know that they are always "in God and God is in them".

7. *Total God-Consciousness* — When every veil of individuality is dissolved, the supremely free soul knows Itself as God.

Though many of these stages are impossible to fully understand unless we experience them for ourselves, it is helpful to contemplate them because such contemplation encourages us to remain steady on the spiritual path and tends to awaken our latent soul memories.

In the body of man there are seven vital places which correspond to these seven levels of awareness. At these vital centers, the physical, astral and causal bodies are connected or *sealed*. On the physical level these places are nerve ganglion and on the astral level they are centers of radiating force. As the physical body is nourished by a flow of life current, as well as by food, so the astral body is vitalized by a steady flow of life force.

THE REVELATION OF ST. JOHN

Let us examine the mystery of St. John's revelation, as recorded in the final book of the New Testament. St. John was in retreat, meditating on the things of the Spirit.

> "I was in the Spirit on the Lord's Day, and heard behind me a great voice, as of a trumpet."
> Revelation 1:10.

Having his attention turned within, St. John intuitively perceived the Aum vibration. It was *behind* him, flowing from Divine realms, from a source beyond the ego sense. Being in tune with the Magnetic Attracting Power, his attention was drawn to the Source. Surrendering to this pull, his inner vision opened and he saw,

The Seven Vital Places in the Body of Man

These vital places are inwardly perceived in deep meditation, as with St. John as recorded in Revelations. Read across for the explanation of lights and functions of each center.

LOCATION	INNER LIGHT & SOUND	FUNCTION	LEVEL OF SOUL AWARENESS
Upper Cerebrum (upper brain)	Clear white light, as of a "thousands suns."	Body Battery, storage area for cosmic energy.	Pure Spirit
Third Eye Center (between eyebrows)	Ring of gold light about a blue field, centered by brilliant white light. (Aum)	Center of will. Conected with the medulla. Center of focus in meditation.	Perfected Being
Cervical Center (in spine at neck)	Multi-colored lights. (Sound of "many waters" - intermingling elements.)	Maintains the balance of ethers in sub-atomic spaces of the body.	Mastership
Dorsal Center (in spine at point between shoulder blades)	Clear blue. (Tinkling bells or gong sound.) Door to the inner worlds.	Controls the movement of vital airs in the body.	State of the "living free."
Lumbar Center (middle spine opposite the navel)	Reddish hues. (Flute-like sounds)	Regulates physical and psychic heat.	Mental Plane
Sacral Center (lower spine)	Various lights; sometimes white crescent. (Harp-like sounds.)	Regulates fluid balance of the body.	Astral Plane
Coccygeal Center (base of spine)	Yellow lights, also, as with the above center, subconscious images are seen reflected at the third eye. (Grating sound or cricket-like sounds.)	Maintains the cohesion of the atomic structure of the body.	Material Plane

with the eye of intuition, both his physical and astral vehicles.

> "And I turned to see the voice that spake with me. And being turned, I saw seven golden candlesticks;
>
> And in the midst of the seven candlesticks one like unto the Son of Man, clothed with a garment down to his foot, and girt about the breasts with a golden girdle.
>
> His head and his hairs were white like wool, as white as snow; and his eyes were as a flame of fire;
>
> And his feet like unto fine brass, as if they burned in a furnace; and his voice as the sound of many waters.
>
> And he had in his right hand seven stars; and out of his mouth went a sharp two edged sword; and his countenance was as the sun shineth in his strength.
>
> And when I saw him, I fell at his feet as dead. And he laid his right hand upon me, saying unto me, Fear not; I am the first and the last:
>
> I am he that liveth, and was dead, and behold, I am alive for evermore. Amen; and I have the keys of hell and death."
>
> 1:12-18.

Seeing his own astral vehicle floating over the prostrate form of his physical body, St. John also saw the centers of vital force in the spinal passageway, and the halo of light surrounding the form. The astral vehicle appeared to be formed much like the physical body, the Son of Man. The brain of the astral body was brilliant white and the third eye center, where positive and negative flows emerge, was as a single flame of fire. A golden aura encircled the form, becoming darker at the feet.

This was the perception of the spiritual body, the astral-causal vehicle which is not dependent upon the physical body, though the physical body is dependent upon it. A sense of immortal life pervaded St. John's consciousness as he was rapt in this inner experience.

SEVEN LEVELS OF SOUL UNFOLDMENT

That he correctly perceived the seven vital places and their energies is clearly revealed in the following:

> "The mystery of the seven stars which thou sawest in my right hand, and the seven golden candlesticks. The seven stars are the angels of the seven churches: and the seven candlesticks which thou sawest are the seven churches." 1:20.

The *angels* are the controlling life currents which flow through the established centers to sustain the bodies. As these centers are opened man's consciousness becomes ever more clear and he is able to understand the seven levels of soul unfoldment and the seven planes of consciousness. This has been termed the ladder of self-realization which man climbs, step by step, from bondage to liberation.

Located throughout the cerebro-spinal nervous system, the vital centers serve as distribution points for the down-flowing life currents. Their locations are: upper cerebrum, body battery or main center of force; third eye center, the point where life forces are distributed through the medulla; cervical center; dorsal center; lumbar center; sacral center and; coccygeal center. The functions of these centers are fully described in the accompanying chart.

There is no need for us to try to awaken these centers by concentration, for as we learn to dwell in the realization of the Presence at all times, the vital forces automatically become activated. There has been much false information published about these vital centers and their corresponding effect on man's consciousness. The most common falsehood is that premature awakening of the vital force leads to sexual excess and emotional imbalance. What happens as a result of the awakening of vital forces in the body is not a negative phenomenon, but rather, some people who have never really been alive before, do not know how to handle their feelings. If we remain steady on the spiritual path, living always in the awarenes of our God-nature, there will never be any problems of any kind for any reason whatsoever.

Due to the movement of vital forces through the system, the contents of the unconscious sometimes float to the surface; giving rise to visions or hallucinations. This is why the master teachers stress the importance of self-realization as the goal, rather than for a person to become intrigued by illusory inner experiences. All perceptions, except the clear awareness of Being, are to be considered as illusory by the sincere seeker of Truth.

St. John, continuing his meditation, going beyond the vision of his lower vehicles, is able to transcend the lesser realms and enter the *door* to the inner kindom:

> "After this I looked, and behold, a door was opened in heaven; and the first voice which I heard was as it were of a trumpet talking with me; which said, Come up hither, and I will shew thee things which must be hereafter.
>
> And immediately I was in the spirit; and, behold, a throne was set in heaven, and one sat on the throne.
>
> And he that sat was to look upon like a jasper and a sardine stone; and there was a rainbow round about the throne, in sight like unto an emerald.
>
> And round about the throne were four and twenty seats: and upon the seats I saw four and twenty elders sitting clothed in white raiment; and they had on their heads crowns of gold.
>
> And out of the thrones proceeded lightnings and thunderings and voices; and there were seven lamps of fire burning before the throne, which are the seven Spirits of God.
>
> And before the throne was a sea of glass like unto crystal: and in the midst of the throne and round about the throne, were four beasts, full of eyes, before and behind." 4:1-6.

SEVEN LEVELS OF SOUL UNFOLDMENT

Passing beyond the levels of material creation, St. John moved in awareness through the *door*, being summoned by the Attracting Current and hearing the Aum continuously. In his awareness as an individualization of Spirit, he perceived the *inner workings* of God. Beholding the true Source, he also perceived the outward radiating flows of force; including the twenty-four active principles of Spirit; which are perceived as the fifteen subtle electricities; five gross elements; plus feeling, ego, mind and intelligence. The soul, detached from creation, can clearly see all forces of which creation is formed.

St. John also perceived the seven major divisions of God involved with creation, as the *Spirits before the throne*, which are responsible for the seven levels of creation. He also understood the nature of the Darkness, the fabric of creation, as the *four beasts;* termed thus because man identified with them instead of with his true nature, is barred from spiritual perception. These four components are, as you will recall; motion, time, space and light particles.

This experience is the true spiritual baptism of man. The Son of Man is the soul identified with these four component parts of the Darkness. The Son of Man is the offspring of the Darkness or the four *origins;* Manus, in Sanskrit, from which the word *man* came. When man's attention is fully interiorized, in deep meditation, he realizes the true Source and Reality of all outer appearances and is at peace within himself; requiring nothing of the outside world for satisfaction or happiness. All of this can be realized while embodied when the doors of perception are cleansed. This is why the spiritual body of man with its electricities and dual poles has been described as a sealed casket of knowledge.

> "And I saw in the right hand of him that sat on the throne a book written within and on the backside, sealed with seven seals."   5:1.

Moving beyond the Darkness, a spiritual aspirant transcends gross creation and becomes free from all involvement with it. Then he awakens to realize his nature as a Son of God.

A RESULT-PRODUCING TECHNIQUE

Here is a technique which can be practiced regularly with satisfying results; it is the method of listening to the cosmic sound current: Aum.

To concentrate properly you will have to find a quiet place, without any disturbing noises. After you have sat in meditation for awhile and are inwardly calm; *flow* the attention to the third eye center and at the same time, listen *within* and *behind* the right ear, if you are right handed. *Within* and *behind* the left ear if you are left handed, because this will be, for you, the side through which a stronger flow of vital force moves.

Sometimes, you might find it more helpful if you hold the ears shut with the thumbs and arrange the fingers comfortably on the forehead. This will give you a psychological advantage as it will direct all of your attention within the skull. Prop your elbows on a table if you will be relaxed and can give full attention to your inner work.

Listening and looking *within*, do not try to visualize anything! Just assume an attitude of receptivity, looking and listening. As you go deep within and the mental activity subsides, you may begin to perceive inner lights; scenes, geometrical patterns, vast expanses of light with various colors shimmering before your inner vision. In the early stages, the pictures are those which are floating up from the subconscious. Patiently try to see through them;—to the Source. After a while the pictures will dissolve and only the multi-colored geometrical patterns, constantly moving, will be viewed. These too, will fade away, leaving you with waves of light, shimmering, expanding, floating before your inner gaze. Try to pierce these lights with your intuition; the lights will become more luminous, brighter and more subtle. Then, you may clearly perceive the clear white light; the "light as of thousand suns". If you see the white light, *surrender yourself to it, melt in it, become it*. At times it may appear as a white silvery moon or a dazzling sun, remaining stationary then vanishing from your sight or breaking up into a scattering of white light particles. This will be due to the restlessness of the mind. By holding your gaze steady, the light will again be seen within.

You may, during your practice, become aware of inner sounds; musical tones, crickets chirping, bells tinkling, or a high pitched continuous sound. Whatever you hear, as with the lights, try to go through the sounds to the Source. In this way you will be led *through* the various astral and causal levels and experience pure Being.

The purpose of listening within and looking within is to enable us to pierce, with the eye of intuition, the veils of consciousness which conceal direct perception of pure Being. We are not to get caught up in the fascinating inner display of lights or the pleasant inner sounds. We are to go beyond them into conscious awareness of our real nature. Like St. John we can, by turning within and following the sound and light, pass through the door to the inner kingdom and understand the nature of God and the workings of creation *as an electrical phenomenon.*

Different sounds and colors correspond to the seven levels of consciousness as centered in the vital places in the body of man. The astral sounds emanate from the vital places because wherever there is vibration there is also light and sound.

THE TUNNEL OF ETERNITY

Here is a visualization technique to help you expand and clear your consciousness. With this method you can learn to move through the third eye gate into the realization of omnipresence. This is the gate in the East, the star followed by all wise men which leads to the awareness of Christ, or Universal Consciousness.

As you flow your attention to the third eye center, the energies in the body will be lifted up and instead of flowing down from the brain, through the nervous system and senses into contact with the world, they will reverse their flow. This reversal of the flow of vital forces will increase your powers of concentration and bring the perception of inner light. Focused at the third eye, you may see the *condensation of the triune nature of God; as golden light which is the light of Aum; as blue light which is the light of Universal Intelligence; as pure white light which is the light of Spirit.* The white light will be encircled by blue which will in turn be encircled by gold. Some see this as though it were about three inches across; others see it as larger or smaller. With the attention and vital force focused at the third eye center, we see the doorway through which life enters the body.

Gently try to merge with the golden light and the Aum, and sense your at-one-ment with all of creation. Then, try to merge with the blue light and sense your at-one-ment with Universal Intelligence. Finally, merge with the white light and experience pure Being. These are the three steps to self-realization after we have transcended the lower realms. *Baptism in the Cosmic Sound Current or Holy Ghost comes first, followed by awakening to the realization of our Christ or Universal Consciousness nature. From there we become aware of our nature as God. So, it is literally true that "none cometh unto the Father except by Me". No one ever realizes the Ultimate Truth without passing from humanhood, through the realm of vibration to Universal Intelligence and then to the realization of Oneness.* The way to self-realization is the *same* for all people regardless of their beliefs or the names by which they refer to God.

As the three vehicles: physical, astral and causal, are interpenetrated, so there are *three* spinal passageways. You know of the spinal cord which passes through the vertebral column. There is also an *astral tube* within the spinal cord and this is the spinal cord of the astral body. Within that is a *subtle tube* or causal spinal cord.

As energies are awakened in the spine and directed upwards, these channels are opened automatically, giving rise to physical sensations of *bliss* and *joy* on the physical level; the awakening of astral senses on the astral level, resulting in *clairvoyance, telepathy,* etc.; and *fine perceptions of the causal realms* when the innermost channel is awakened. Complete awakening and regeneration enables man, while embodied, to know the truth about all levels of creation and that which is *beyond* creation.

As a result of our steady contemplation of the inner Light, we experience a feed-down of Light and Power that takes place on subtle levels and results in transformation and purification of all levels of consciousness, which make up our nature.

There are five stages of conditioning in the consciousness of man; *dark; partially awakened; already on the spiritual path; devoted to the Supreme Reality* and; *illumined.* Man is thus classified and his evolutionary status is determined accordingly.

In man whose consciousness is darkened or clouded, we find only interest in material things. A person at this stage is best fitted to serve others who are more enlightened and to follow their lead in all important matters. Though there are millions of people at this stage of unfoldment on the planet today, during the last Dark Age cycle the majority of people were at this level.

Becoming a little enlightened, man begins to compare his experiences in the waking state to the experiences of the dream state and from this begins to realize the essential dream-nature of creation. At this time he awakens a bit and begins to search out the truth of life in order to clear his doubts. If he is wise he will seek out the guidance of enlightened men and learn from them how to prepare himself for greater understanding. He becomes steady on the path.

Then, such a person becomes devoted to the spiritual path and begins to put order in his environment, trying to work in harmony with the Divine so as not to create any new complications for himself or for others. The end result is that he experiences enlightment and becomes a knower of truth.

The way to reach a better understanding is to associate with people who are wise. Reverent association with those who know more than we, invariably results in our being lifted to their level.

CHAPTER EIGHT

Exploring the Inner Worlds

Exploring the Inner Worlds

Whole new worlds come into view as we become aware of deeper and more subtle areas of consciousness. We gain easy access to the contents of the subconscious mind, understand scriptures and the secrets of nature, have vivid and meaningful dreams, learn how to leave the physical body at will, and roam in realms of light.

All of the experiences and perceptions of which I now write will come to every spiritual aspirant in time, and there is no need for anyone to try for these experiences. I explain them here only so you will know what is happening when you begin to have unusual inner experiences. If we try always to be anchored in the realization of God, we can then be self-contained and objective regardless of what we perceive.

One of the earliest happenings for the average person on the path is that he becomes more aware of the thoughts, feelings and intentions of other people. He becomes telepathic. He also becomes aware of the inner guidance and, at times, is even able to *preview* the future. He just seems to *know* what is going to happen.

The dream experience also becomes more vivid. In ordinary sleep we escape from the pressing demands of the world for a while and allow for inner adjustments to be made so that we can once again face life on this plane. Some sleep researchers today are of the opinion that ordinary dreaming is the mind's way of filing and arranging the mental and emotional impressions gathered during the waking hours. It is known that all people, and animals, dream even when they are not aware of the process. An examination of the brain waves, the flickering of the eyelids and breathing tempo reveals this.

There is a way to predetermine your dreams; as you relax prior to going to sleep, visualize a scene you want to dream about. As you hold this picture steady and sink into sleep, the mental picturing will transform into a dream experience. As you go to sleep, hold the thought that you will be aware when you dream. In due time, perhaps not at the first few attempts, you will suddenly be aware that you are dreaming; as a participant or a bystander. At this time, you can either watch the dream sequence; alter it by an act of will, stop it, run it backwards or dissolve it; whatever you elect to do. If you are dreaming in black and white you can, by an act of will, dream in full color and with a sense of reality bordering on your waking experience. When you awaken, if you will compare your attitude during the dream with life as it appears about you in this three-dimensional realm, you will see that this waking experience is just as much a dream as was the sleeping dream. *You are the eternal dreamer* and the pictures appearing about you are constantly changing. Seeing the dream-nature of life you attain greater freedom.

When we are awake, perceiving through the senses, we are working through the physical body. When we sleep (or use will and imagination) we function through the astral body. When we are in deep dreamless sleep, deep meditation or in abstract thought, we function through the subtle causal vehicle.

Now, not all dreams are true astral experiences; that is, *out-of-the-body* experiences. Most dreams are merely subconscious activities. Some however, are significant. Sometimes while we dream, we act out our suppressed desires; we do things we would like to do in the waking state but for some reason we cannot do. It is not unusual for a poor man to dream that he is rich, a spiritually impoverished person to dream that he is enlightened, or a sexually repressed person to delight in the most uninhibited relationships. In these ways our secret urges are fulfilled on the subconscious level and the pressure is relieved, which might otherwise build up and result in neurotic or psychotic behavior. Of course, to purposely seek fulfillment, through dreams, and avoid creative living in this world is a form of escapism and is unwise.

It is quite probable that we, at times, leave the physical body during sleep and visit distant places in order to communicate with others. One should be extremely careful, however, not to become fascinated with this kind of experience and be led into a life of illusion. I, for instance, have had on rare occasions, vivid dream-like experiences in which I found myself talking with enlightened teachers; always with benefit. In this manner I have communed with Yogananda, Sri Yukteswar and other masters. There is always the possibility of wishful thinking involved in such experiences, or perhaps; Divine Mind, to meet our need, forms as certain personalities on the dream or vision level so that we can receive the guidance we need.

Some years ago, I *felt* an overshadowing presence of Sri Yukteswar, and with it came the strong feeling to write a book; a commentary on the *Yoga Sutras of Patanjali*. Days passed, and the feeling continued. So I set about the task. I found my inspiration high and the creative work flowed easily. As a result, in short order, the manuscript was published as *This is Reality* and has blessed countless thousands of lives. Now, I do not really know if Sri Yukteswar actually prompted me to write the book. I do know that I have always had a natural ability to explain the teachings of the East in modern English and have also known this to be one of my major responsibilities in this incarnation.

A brother disciple of mine, Mr. J. J. Lynn, was highly advanced spiritually. Shortly before he left this world he developed a brain tumor which, even after surgery, made meditation difficult because of the pain. Once in meditation, Babaji appeared to him and showed him how to leave the body consciously and meditate while encased in his astral form. In this way the physical body was not a hindrance.

On another occasion, Mr. Lynn awakened in the middle of the night; instead of the perception of light and bliss which had been his for years, there was only the sensation of darkness and depression. He directed his attention to the third eye center. After what seemed to be a long time, a small white point of light appeared there. Suddenly, he *became* that light; gradually the light expanded and, atom by atom, it seemed as though his entire body was reconstructed. But, the experience did not end there; he continued to expand as light, becoming the physical universe, the astral and causal worlds, and eventually the *totality of Being*. After many hours in this transcendental experience, he came back to body consciousness and opened his eyes; Babaji, Lahiri Mahasaya, Sri Yukteswar and Yogananda were standing in light bodies beside his bed.

Another brother disciple, who is yet with us in this world and who prefers to remain anonymous, has always been a creative and inventive genius. He is an executive in a midwestern city. He told me personally that in years past when he was faced with a seeming impossible problem, he would meditate. It was not unusual for him to see, with his eyes open, *a bright light appear in the room and form into a radiant being* who would then advise him correctly. After his mission was fulfilled the master would vanish. My brother disciple said "They, (the masters) don't fool around; they get right to the point. And, the longer they have been liberated the more beautiful they are."

There is a difference between visions and clairvoyant perceptions. Visions are conscious dreams, projected from the mind of the person who sees them and colored by his subconscious conditionings. Thus a Christian frequently beholds one of the saints of Christendom, or Jesus; and people of the orient see the saints with whom they are familiar. A vision is a mental projection, formed of the individual's mind-stuff, and can have, if it is a true superconscious vision, very real meaning. On the other hand, because subconscious conditionings are present, visions are often misinterpreted. On a lower level they are hallucinations which are subconsciously produced as compensation for personal inadaquacies. Mystics teach that visions should not be pursued as this is evidence of outward seeking and can lead to disillusionment.

Clairvoyant perception of subtle realms or of persons in subtle bodies, is different. We actually see what is there; not a production of our own mind. But, even clairvoyant perceptions are not to be sought because, again, it is evidence of lack of self-completeness. If such perceptions come and they are meaningful, we can take them in stride.

We all unfold in different ways. I seldom see auras and never see visions. But, my dreams are luminous and sometimes transcendental in character. Also, my sense of knowing is highly refined. All of my life I have *just known* things which were later verified. In this manner I have known my life's destiny, the difference between fact and fiction in my quest for Truth and even, to a great extent, what the future holds for me and those close to me. Knowing directly the truth about anything is superior to perceiving glimpses of the truth. Many people can see auras, travel astrally, read the future and the past; and still are not enlightened.

Astral projection can be accomplished at will by anyone who is willing to practice it. Astral travel should not be done just out of idle curiosity. But, if it happens spontaneously, we at least know beyond a shadow of a doubt that we do survive the physical body. Many people find it difficult to leave the physical body consciously because of a deep-seated fear. The physical body has become, for them, an anchor to the gross world. It is their home for the duration of this incarnation. Some people are even hesitant to leave when their time is up because they have

EXPLORING THE INNER WORLDS

learned to adjust to this world and are unsure of the next.

My first conscious exit from this body was some years ago. I had been traveling and lecturing for several days and was physically tired. While resting on the bed in the guest room at the home of friends, I reclined on my back, a bit tense, finding sleep difficult. Suddenly, there was a pressure at the base of the skull and I felt myself rising, feet first, then the rest of my body, from the bed. The head disconnected last and I floated to the ceiling, fully conscious. *Willing* to turn over, I did, and remained at ceiling level, looking down at the bed, clearly aware of the dimly lit room and the noises beyond it. Then, just as I had ascended, I descended; head first, the rest of my astral form fitting into my physical body. I sat up, clearly aware, pondered the experience for a few moments, then stretched out and went to sleep.

Here is something to remember; astral projection is just one form of projection. We can also leave both the physical and astral vehicles and function as a point of awareness, traveling at will through space. Once during meditation, I was shocked back to surface consciousness by a loud noise in the building. Turning my attention within again with deep concentration, I found myself to be an unit of awareness; aware of I, only. I had *spherical vision*. I could *see* in all directions but I was in space; distant lights glimmered, all was serene and quiet in the soft-blue light. The memory of this vivid experience as pure awareness, without any restricting bodies, has never left me.

ASTRAL TELEVISION

As we remember that in the transcendental experience we are above the time-space order, the realm of relativity, we realize that we can, because of our omnipresent nature, become aware of anything, anywhere, anytime. By closing our eyes and shutting off the awareness of the external world, we can look within to the third eye center and *will* to see any one and any place we desire. And there, within, we will *see* what we want to see. This form of astral television enables us to tune in to any person or any happening, present, past or future.

If you have a reason for contacting another person who lives at a distance, do this: Sit quietly, with your attention centered within at the third eye, the *cosmic reflecting mirror*. Desire to see the person of your choice and you will see him, as he is, before your inner vision. You can, if you so desire, also know anything about people, their feelings, problems, present circumstances; whatever. If your responsibility is to help them, *inwardly see them as they are, in Truth, as enlightened Sons of God*. In this way you help clear the darkness from their consciousness through the power of your superior realization.

LEAVING THE BODY AND HIGHER REALMS

Sooner or later we all must leave the physical body. We should not desire to leave until our reason for being here has been fulfilled, otherwise, we will retain subconscious karmic patterns which may result in our early return. But, when the time comes to leave, we can make the exit easily if we know the secret.

After years of regular meditation we learn to know ourselves as pure Spirit. We learn to withdraw the attention and vital forces into the third eye and upper cerebrum. When the soul leaves the body at the final moment it leaves through the spinal passageway, ascending the seven centers as it moves out, withdrawing the astral body and all of the vital forces with it.

Some people who are involved in accidents are thrown out of the body quickly and find themselves standing to one side of the body or perhaps hovering over the body,

EXPLORING THE INNER WORLDS

but they are still tuned in to the physical plane. In time, they either go to sleep and later find themselves awakening on an astral plane, or they awaken yet more and lose awareness of the physical realms as their clairvoyant sight becomes developed. If a person remains aware of the physical world after he leaves the body, he finds that he is earth-bound; aware of people here who are not aware of his presence. Some people also leave the body while in deep sleep, in sickness or old age. They have dreams and in time, awaken to an astral plane which is consistent with their level of understanding. Remaining there for a while, they again go to sleep and incarnate into a flesh body on the planet earth; or on any one of a number of physical planets in the galaxy.

There is a way to leave consciously at physical death. As a result of proper meditation we learn to realize our nature as Light and Life, then the exit from the body becomes a simple thing. Enlightened initiates know ahead of time when they will leave this world and they prepare themselves for the event. Not only do they condition themselves through deep meditation but they also *neutralize the last tracings of karma and complete their duties in this world. Entering meditation they plunge into the Light and experience the Great Oneness.*

The average person, leaving consciously, but against his will, as the life currents are pulled up the spine and out of the brain, finds that he *relives the major emotional experiences of his life on earth.* For some, this can be a traumatic experience as they are faced with the playback of their misdeeds, failures, frustrations and painful moments. At this stage, many are self-judged by their reaction to what they behold. Possessed by fear, overcome by shame and a feeling of unworthiness they go to sleep, to dream fitful dreams. They move into the astral realms in this condition of consciousness and spend some time working through subconscious dream experiences before they make their adjustment and awaken to the astral realms.

Others, who are God-tuned, rise out of the body with a sense of elation and freedom. *They are able to observe the motion-picture-like sequence of memories with detachment and non-reaction.* Some just *step free* of the body without going through the confusion of millions of mental pictures and the corresponding feelings.

While on the astral level, a person either continues his unfoldment or simply enjoys himself for a while, before incarnating once more. Many people find their astral experience to be very similar to earth experience. They live on an astral planet with others of a similar level of consciousness, and enter into social activities.

Persons endowed with a strong urge for self-realization continue their spiritual practices and shed desires and urges which tie them to the lower astral spheres and move on to more subtle ones. These souls do not have to return to the physical universe. They work for greater understanding and gradually move from the astral realms to the subtler causal realms.

The astral cosmos is larger than the physical cosmos. There we find planets and solar systems, inhabited by a great variety of men and women, the majority of them being banded together on the particular planet which agrees with their level of understanding. As on earth, in the astral realms we are drawn to people who have spiritual and mental attitudes which are similar to ours.

Advanced astral inhabitants can travel from planet to planet in masses of light if they so desire. The colors in the more refined astral spheres are brilliant. People communicate telepathically as well as verbally. Their bodies are sustained by a direct flow of vital force, even though they can, if they wish, eat food which grows there. The personal relationship still exists on the astral. People enjoy each other's company and men and women mate and raise families. Their children are born from the higher astral realms or from the subtle causal realms.

Just as in this world, souls incarnate into flesh bodies and then depart for a while to the astral realms; so on the astral levels, souls incarnate from the causal, dwell in astral bodies for a time, then depart to the causal realms once again. Finally, they graduate from the astral realms and remain on the causal plane and from there, work out their causal karma in order to transcend even that rarified plane of creation.

No fixed time exists for a person's stay on the astral levels. If the subconscious pull to earth is strong, the soul only remains for a short time, even though a few years of earth time can be experienced as hundreds of years of astral time; just as we can experience what seems to be many hours of dreaming when, in fact, only a few seconds or a few minutes have passed. Souls which leave the physical plane, with an attachment to the planet earth, during a descending Dark Age Cycle, often remain on the astral planes for hundreds of years until the earth-cycle is again suitable for their re-entry. Thus, it is not difficult to understand that many souls on earth now have not been here since the times of ancient Atlantis and past Golden Ages.

There are gross astral spheres, not much different in appearance to the physical planes, where people are selfish and wrongly motivated. On these levels wars exist which are more devastating than earthly wars, because the inhabitants know how to use the power of thought and vibration; and this ability is now coming on the scene on earth. There are celestial realms also, where highly developed souls reside. These realms are veritable heavens and the masses of people are forever aware of their God-nature. On these and all levels, great spiritual teachers work as saviors to redeem souls, even as such teachers work here on earth and throughout space. The activity of soul-enlightenment goes on endlessly, on all levels of creation, until all souls enter through the door to the inner kingdom and know themselves in God.

When we leave this world we go to an astral realm of our desire. If we think and feel that we are unworthy, we move into a gloomy realm inhabited by negative and pessimistic people, the *hell* envisioned by so many. If we yearn for association with members of our family we move into a realm where people are family-conscious and, for the most part, no more enlightened than they were on earth. If we contemplate the realms of light or desire the companionship of celestial beings, this is our after-death experience.

Incarnating once again, because we go to sleep on the astral realm and because physical birth is somewhat traumatic, we lose the memory of immediate past astral experiences. If we are nearly enlightened and elect to incarnate, even though the memory is partially blotted out we soon begin to become aware of our real nature and fleeting glimpses, brought up from the storehouse of memory, begin to make their appearance on the screen of our inner consciousness.

When a person near to you is leaving the body, it is no time for weeping or showing outward signs of grief because this only confuses the departing soul. It is better to allow the person to be alone, in a quiet environment. Or sit at the bedside and read accounts of celestial after-earth-life experience.

A practice is known by the true initiates; *to daily enter the awareness of the inner Light during meditation, and while going to sleep, so it becomes an easy thing to do.* Then, at the final moment, a person can retire within and meditate and move out consciously and easily. At such times it is not unusual for a teacher from the astral realms, summoned by an intuitive call, to come to the departing soul, usher him into the astral world, introduce him around and make him familiar with the new environment.

Though some astrally embodied people can, through the use of intuition, pierce the veil between the worlds and see the inhabitants of the physical realms, enlightened souls do not do this unless they have a specific reason for doing so. And, conversely, people in the physical world should not try to make contact with souls which have departed to other realms. Such souls left this world because they had business elsewhere and should not be pulled back merely to satify our idle curiosity or to assuage our grief. If we are curious or grief-stricken it shows that we are not properly self-realized and we should spend more time studying the great truths and seeking deeper understanding.

For the most part, even enlightened teachers who have gone on to the astral and causal realms, do not directly communicate with people on earth, because they have finished their work here and are busy elsewhere. They usually leave trained disciples behind on the planet to carry on in their spirit.

On the spiritual path, we continue to make progress; incarnating time after time, moving ever onwards. Even if we do not experience complete enlightment in the present incarnation, no gain is ever lost. We will continue to unfold on the astral planes and, should we incarnate on earth again, we will begin the spiritual quest at an earlier age than we did in this present incarnation. True, some people become temporarily diverted but, eventually, by comparing mere sense experiences with the bliss of spiritual unfoldment they return to serious study and make rapid progress.

CHAPTER NINE

The Revelation of the Supreme Self

The Revelation of the Supreme Self

Great ability is realized by a person who becomes God-conscious. *Realizing his nature as God, a person is able to understand and able to do whatever he feels led to do.* All this is possible because of deep realization and pure concentration.

We know that the physical world operates under the fundamental laws of relativity and duality. God is appearing as separate and diverse manifestations of creation. Electricity, for instance, is a phenomenon of repulsion and attraction; its electrons and protons are electrical opposites. The atom is, itself, like our earth, a magnet with positive and negative poles. No law of physics, chemistry or any other science is free from inherent contrasted principles.

Science must deal with the nature of creation as it is, therefore, objective investigators can only probe so far in their quest for final answers. The great sages declare that man's major goal in life is to learn to overcome the pairs of opposites which are basic to the relative world. The only way to transcend relativity is to become God-conscious. "Afterwards he brought me to the gate, even the gate that looketh toward the east; and his voice was like a noise of many waters: and the earth shined with his glory." (Ezekiel 43: 1-2) Being lifted into a new dimension of consciousness, Ezekiel perceived the *cosmic vibration and the nature of light which is the basis of creation.*

Light passes freely through the vacuum of space, requiring no material media. Light remains the most subtle of all natural phenomena. As far as we know, light is the most nearly fixed manifestation in the universe. Einstein, in his Unified Field Theory, embodied in a mathematical formula the laws of gravitation and electromagnetism. Many scientists today declare that the atom is not only energy but is basically *mind-stuff*. The electron has a dual nature, partaking of the characteristics of both a particle and a wave, the latter giving the electron the characteristic of light.

To a person in meditation who perceives the true nature of creation as light, there is no difference between the light rays composing water, earth, metals or fleshly bodies. *In this realization all delusions are destroyed and the liberated soul sees the universe as masses of light.*

We have discussed the Darkness before in this text. The Old Testament prophets referred to the Darkness as *Satan*, which in Hebrew means "the adversary". The Greek Testament, as an equivalent, uses *diabolus* or *devil*. These are terms for the Darkness, the medium from which creation is formed. Jesus knew that a person involved with this fabric of nature was deluded. The "works of the devil, the Darkness" are destroyed through self-realization.

For a God-conscious person, free of ego, it is the most natural thing in the world to effortlessly conform with right action. In Emerson's words, all great ones become "not virtuous, but Virtue; then is the end of creation answered and God is well pleased". A God-conscious person can influence other's minds or even the course of events because of universal sympathy. Being in tune with all of creation, a master can, if he so desires, take a hand in controlling any phase of creation.

Only in certain instances, however, do the masters use their power of will to influence natural happenings. They usually prefer to let the chain of cause and effect neutralize opposite forces in nature and in the lives of human beings.

In an earlier chapter you learned about meditation and the secret of true concentration. *Whatever we concentrate upon, with the desire to know the truth about, we can identify with and understand.* By anchoring our attention to any problem or any facet of nature, with the desire to know, the truth will be revealed intuitively.

Transcending the mind we enter into the secret place and know what no mortal can hope to know.

For instance, by contemplating on the nature of God we begin to understand what God is; by contemplating on the nature of the soul we come to understand that we are rays of God; by contemplating on the sense of separation, or ego, we erase the concept of separateness and know ourselves as God.

Likewise, by contemplating on the intention of people we learn to bypass their verbal efforts and see into their hearts and minds. By contemplating the past we recall previous embodiments and, if we go back far enough, we remember our Divine nature, as it was in the beginning. By contemplating our inner nature we become aware of our personal destiny. And, so it goes, we can know whatever we want to know by *accepting* the possibility and by *contemplating* properly.

Of course, it is most desirable to contemplate the nature of Reality and become God-conscious, because this will solve all of our problems. We soon learn that "My grace is sufficient for thee".

Now, the various abilities which come can be obstacles to self-realization and we should use them only for the highest good of mankind and according to our inner guidance. We should never use higher powers to demonstrate our superior ability, to attract attention or to take advantage of others. Only a liberated person is able to make use of the supernatural powers which come as a result of self-realization. Of course, we can use our increased awareness and natural abilities to perform more constructively in the world but never for any selfish purpose.

Eight powers are claimed by advanced initiates. Let us consider them carefully:

1. THE POWER OF MINUTENESS

This gives a person the ability to see into the heart of the smallest particle of matter and therefore enables him to understand the true nature of the Darkness, the fabric of nature, so that he can overcome the world. With insight we can clearly grasp the interworkings of force, time, space and light particles and by so doing, rise above their influence.

2. THE POWER OF MAGNITUDE

A liberated person can become cosmic conscious and realize his nature as *all there is*. He is able to know himself as the ocean and the wave; as transcendental Spirit and as Spirit manifested as creation. Even while working through a body he knows himself to be Universal Spirit temporarily focused through the body.

3. THE POWER OF GRAVITY

Understanding the nature of the outflowing force, inertia, man is able to anchor himself to causal, astral or physical creation in order to fulfill his destiny. He does this, as the masters do, by a subconscious act of will. In this way he can remain in the body for as long as he likes, to work out karma or, if he is free of karma, to work for the good of mankind. His grasp on the world is purely voluntary.

4. THE POWER OF LIGHTNESS

By contemplating the Magnetic Attraction, a person can find release from the pull of inertia or gravity and transcend the world. He does not need to be held here against his will. There are records of some saints having experienced levitation due to this power and there are said to be some masters who do not leave footprints even in soft material.

5. THE POWER TO ATTAIN ANY OBJECTIVE

Now we come to practical abilities. With an understanding of the laws of nature and with the full use of our creative talents we should be able to do whatever we feel led to do in this world. The secret of attaining any objective, whatever it might be, is to inwardly see yourself in the possession of it with such certainty that outer conditions adjust themselves to make it possible. It is a matter of properly using creative visualization.

6. THE POWER OF IRRESISTIBLE WILL

Once we know we are right, regardless of our venture, with the power of irresistible will, we can easily move through any barrier. We function in an appearance-world; therefore nothing in the world is stable. All is subject to change. Irresistible will or God-will, makes anything possible.

7. THE POWER TO BE CREATIVE

In this world, with creative power, we can express without restriction. an unending flow of God-force moves through us and into expression. In the relative world we are the only instruments through which the Infinite can express on the highest level. Therefore, we have a great responsibility and a great opportunity if we will take advantage of it. It is claimed that highly self-realized souls can actually, through the use of will and creative power, produce whole universes.

8. THE POWER TO CONTROL CREATION

Through inner visualization we can establish the picture of what we want to see reflected in the outer worlds and it will manifest because of the law of creation. Remember, the universes were projected by the will of God; so we can project modifications in nature by using the same method. As we ignore appearances and inwardly establish the picture of what we want to manifest; and hold it steady, the picture moves through the causal realm, builds up a magnetic force-field and materializes on the physical level.

If our motives are not pure, if we are selfish, we use this power destructively as in the case of black magicians. If we use it with good intentions, but not always with wisdom, we are white magicians. Initiates use this power for good only.

DEGREES OF GOD-CONSCIOUSNESS

It is obvious that there are degrees of God-consciousness. For instance, we soon become aware, after we have been on the path for a while, of an intuitive sensing of God. We know God is real but we are not fully aware of the nature of God. This is a beginning. With proper meditation and by observing the rules of spiritual living, we gradually grow out of the sense of mortality and into a greater realization of Reality. It is not uncommon to experience quick insights which have to be established in our consciousness and pattern of living. Sometimes, it seems that we are not making any progress at all and these are occasions when we must be patient with the inner knowledge that this is a time when we are working through deepseated subconscous patterns and, if we persist in faith, before long the Light will dawn. We should not suppose that the attainment of God-realization is an overnight process or merely a matter of a few weeks or months. Of course, dramatic insights can come but we must allow time for the new realization to filter through our consciousness and transform and purify our nature.

Patience is necessary on the spiritual path. With an inward knowing of our true nature we must let the organism become refined, and the feeling nature purified, through the action of Divine Life in and through us. In this way the subconscious is cleared of the distortions and obstacles to self-realization; *hatred, shame, fear, grief, condemnation, race prejudice, family pride and the smug sense of self-righteousness.* Even all theories, concepts, systems and methods must eventually be discarded. There is a critical phase of self-realization when we must stop trying to attain and awaken to the fact that we are now God expressing. Any effort to attain is evidence of our belief that we are separate from God.

As a result of pure motives we cease to create new karmic patterns; by remaining neutral and God-centered both in good times and bad, we work out existing karmic patterns; and by meditating deeply and letting God-consciousness determine our life we clear out deep-seated karmic patterns which reside in the recesses of the subconscious mind as minute tracings or impressions.

This is why an initiate, even though possessed of great ability and supernatural power hardly ever uses his ability and power. Only when inwardly directed to do so will he exercise his influence to alter the trend of events. Usually, an initiate rests in the full realization of God and prays for nothing except greater realization, content to let the outer life fall into place in line with ever-deeper realizations. An initiate's only desire is to let God's will be done. And, of course, this means that the welfare of man is assured.

There is no definite pattern for individual awakening. Some people gain inward realization of God in deep meditation, but lose this awareness when they cease their meditation practice. Others, who do not meditate very much, have occasional flashes of insight during the day when the mind is calm. Regardless of how the awareness of God comes, we are to gradually maintain the awareness at all times, even when involved in the fulfillment of our daily responsibilities. There are two stages of God-realization; the lower stage and the higher. The lower stage is fleeting and passes, with only a memory of how it was. The higher stage is when the initiate is always aware of his divine nature and sees everything in creation, always, as God expressing. For the person who is established in God-realization there is nothing more to attain, the effort to seek God ceases.

But there are deeper and deeper realizations even after the attainment of the higher stage of God-realization. This is why mystics refer to God as *ever-new* and *ever-desirable*. As long as there is evidence of individu-

THE REVELATION OF THE SUPREME SELF

ality there must be deeper realizations until the awareness of pure Being is experienced.

It is not necessary for us to experience rapture, dramatic inner happenings or blinding ecstasies. Some people do have a wide variety of psychic experiences and others simply awaken to clear awareness, bypassing many of the planes of consciousness along the way. All experiences of light, feeling, movement in subtle worlds and so on, are really illusory experiences. As initiates, we should desire to go beyond all lesser levels and planes and become anchored in God, so that we can work consciously from that level.

In occult literature there is a story which tells of a man who was invited to visit his king at a certain hour on a certain day. Arriving early the man wandered about the palace gardens and became so enthralled with the beauty of it that he missed his appointment with the king. Had he met the king on time he could have undoubtedly had access to the palace grounds at any time thereafter.

If we are dedicated enough to realize the Supreme Self, we can, if any desire is left to do so, have access to the outer realms at will. Life in one incarnation is short, therefore we should make every effort to become God-conscious as soon as we can. It would be a pity to let this golden opportunity pass by and have to continue in the helpless round of action and reaction, birth and death, incarnation after incarnation.

My guru, Yogananda, told me, *"No matter what others do or do not do; if no one else makes the effort to attain self-realization, you must!"* He always stressed that our full attention should be one-pointed and never-swerving until the goal was reached. We can do so much more for mankind after we attain wisdom. The average good person, even with pure intentions, does not always know what is best for himself or for others. But, a person who is functioning as a visible manifestation of God on earth, as a knower of Truth, is the greatest blessing. Behind this world of space-time, interpenetrating it, is the creative purpose of God. When we understand the great design and are content to serve it, every act becomes a symbol of something which is far beyond itself.

In the Bhagavad Gita, Krishna wisely instructs Arjuna, "He who works for Me, who looks upon Me as his goal, who worships Me, free from attachment, he who is free of all enmity to all creatures, he realizes my true nature." *Thus is the revelation of the Supreme Self accomplished.*

CHAPTER TEN

The Final Perfection

The Final Perfection

I will now explain how you can learn to live at all times in God-consciousness: the *Master-consciousness*. An initiate is a person who sees solutions instead of problems and who moves freely through life, unmoved by the shadows and appearances about him which threaten those who are yet dreaming the mortal dream.

The great secret of perfect living is to be forever anchored in God and to work from that level of awareness. If, at times, you are confused or baffled, meditate for a while and regain the proper perspective about life before moving ahead. Life does not have to be a struggle, a matter of continual overcoming. Life can be free and glorious when we know the truth about it.

There are five causes for all human problems. Understanding these causes and being able to successfully eradicate them, you will not have to be limited, distressed or in pain. You will not have to pray to overcome undesirable conditions; you will merely learn to see through them. Instead of wrestling with outer effects you will be able to work with inner causes.

1. LACK OF SPIRITUAL UNDERSTANDING

This is the basic problem confronting the human race. Lacking realization of the true nature of God, man becomes identified with the Darkness, as we have explained, and becomes deluded. In this deluded condition he is liable to experience an infinite number of problems because he is "just being human". He can succeed sometimes and he can fail, he can enjoy good health or he can get sick, he can be accident-free or accident prone, he can be dominated by the *will to live* or by the *will to die*. He is, in effect, at the mercy of the forces in nature and of his own inner subconscious conditionings.

The only solution to this problem is to yearn for spiritual awakening, follow a positive path of action and meditate. When we become God-conscious, the dream vanishes and we are free, able to live as Sons of God.

2. AVOIDING RESPONSIBILITY

As a result of consciously or unconsciously avoiding responsibility for our thoughts, feelings and actions, we learn to survive in the world by having others take care of us and provide for us. Any person, who is in earnest, can learn to think in a positive manner, engage in constructive action and assume personal responsibility. We do not have to be dependent upon other people's charity; we can find our own place in life and work in harmony with the Divine Plan.

3. SELF PITY

There are some people who feel unworthy of the blessings of life because of their shortcomings or because of the mistakes they have made in life. Because of self-pity they punish themselves. They harbor guilt, regret, resentment and a negative self-image and therefore subconsciously create conditions about them which reflect these mental and emotional distortions. They make themselves pay for real or imagined wrong actions and thoughts. God does not punish man. Man punishes himself, often out of proportion to the reason.

4. ATTRACTING ATTENTION TO ONESELF

Because of a basic insecurity, some people consciously or subconsciously create problems in order to attract attention to themselves. They silently say, "Look at me, look how miserable I am." On the spiritual path we should not desire the praise or the criticism of man. We should mature and be concerned only with living in tune with the Infinite.

5. CONTROLLING OTHER PEOPLE

Again, because of insecurity or a morbid sense of power, some people use their weaknesses and problems to make others sympathetic so they can control them. We frequently make the mistake of giving in to the whims of problem-centered people and thereby reinforce their childish tendencies. The way out of this situation is to grant all people total freedom and to find our own place in life so that the right people are drawn into our lives without our having to manipulate and control anyone.

If you will analyze the failures of most people, their illnesses, personality problems and seeming limitations, you will find one or a combination of several of the above mentioned causes behind the conditions. There are some people who are natural "losers" in life because of their subconscious will to fail. There are others who are natural "winners" because they have a vital zest for life and they want to unfold their true potential. We should all be "winners". We should all learn to apply the basic metaphysical principles of *synchronized thinking, feeling and behavior* and put order in our lives. We should all desire to awaken spiritually and transcend human consciousness, which is the only *permanent cure* for all of man's ailments.

THE SON OF MAN vs. THE SON OF GOD

Which will it be? The decision is ours to make. Shall we remain deluded as all Sons of Man are, or shall we awaken and be knowers of truth as the Sons of God know it? *We have the choice.* It was given to us with the unveiling of intellect which enables us to discern that which is essential to our well-being as in contrast to that which is non-essential.

If we persist in believing that we must work out our karma over a period of incarnations, if we persist in selfish desiring, we will be chained to matter for a seemingly endless period of time. Jesus stated a truth, "If you believe not that I am He, then you will die in your sins." In other words, *if we will not awaken and accept ourselves as enlightened beings we will continue in the mortal dream, in darkness, and die to this world in that deluded condition.*

THE FINAL PERFECTION

Some newcomers on the path give in too easily by assuming, "All this philosophy is too deep for me!" They forget that because they are rays of God they can also be knowers of the Ultimate Truth. This ability is inherent in our nature. Deep within us we already know the Truth; it is but a matter of awakening to the realization of it. I know from experience, as well as observation, that if man will but contemplate the truth of life, as set forth in this book and in the sacred writings of the world, with the attitude of being able to know, the slumbering soul consciousness will awaken and man will rise through layers of consciousness until he reaches the surface where all is bright, shining and forever self-complete.

We should desire nothing, as initiates, except the will of God in our lives. We should never give in to the temptation to pray for, or visualize, specific outer effects. We are not to make anything happen. We are to clear our perceptions so that we can see the World of Reality actively manifested in this world. There is a subtle shading of difference between the metaphysical way of life and the true spiritual way of life.

"But," the question comes, "if I don't make anything happen, if I don't strongly desire anything, how will I get by, how will I be provided for in this world?" The answer is this: When we live in the master-consciousness, situations externalize from within us in proper order and for the highest good of all concerned.

For instance, when we feel led to embark upon a certain venture, we do not have to make anything happen; we have but to rest in the conviction that it is already as good as materialized and then let outer happenings take care of themselves. Yes, we have to do our part, in line with our inner guidance, but with the inner knowing that the same Intelligence which prompted the inner picture is even now bringing forth the means for the fulfillment of the desire. *The Divine urge and the fulfillment are one and the same.*

God-consciousness is our natural condition. Deluded consciousness is a perversion of the Real. Therefore, when we are in our right mind, the illumined mind, we are transformed because we are renewed moment by moment. Health, prosperity, creative expression, harmonious relationships with people; all these things are natural to a person who is divinely awakened and moves in his right place in life, by grace. We do not have to specifically pray for or visualize health, prosperity or anything else. We have but to see through the distortions in mind and consciousness which prevent the natural unfoldment of life. Instead of *overcoming*, an initiate *sees through appearances* and gets behind the scenes into the realm of cause and works only from that level.

An initiate *translates* outer appearances. When faced with a problem or a barrier we should do this: Be reminded that everything in manifestation is consciousness appearing; see the condition as it *appears to be* and recognize the inner cause which is sustaining it; *see through* the distorted belief and *accept the* natural condition of freedom and right action; then *act* from that moment as though the new picture were real and the distorted shadow picture unreal.

Can God be limited? Can God be sick, impoverished, lonely, griefstricken or fearful? Of course not. *As a Son of God, an illumined ray of Light, there are no restrictions and no barriers to contain you.* Think about it. Contemplate it. Let your intuition reveal the truth about your real nature and your certain destiny.

If outer conditions do not yield immediately, be patient; know that with the changing of inner cause you have cut off the roots of the distorted outer picture and it will collapse of its own accord. Outer conditions are reflections of inner pictures. When we change the inner picture, the outer condition, being but a reflection on the screen of time and space, will inevitably be transformed just as light banishes darkness.

THE FINAL PERFECTION

In dealing with other people, separate, in your mind, the Real Person from the temporary conditionings of the subconscious. No one in this world is evil, malicious, sick, impoverished or ignorant; all appearances are due to the soul's wrong identification. The deluded soul identifies with creation and builds up a complex web of karmic conditionings which then reflect as outer conditions. But, the soul, the Son of God, is ever perfect and unconditioned. So, we never condemn anyone and we never try to improve them, even a little bit, in the absolute sense. We merely see them as enlightened beings, even as we are, and bring forth this awareness of Self, which will automatically free them.

This means we must see with the eye of the soul, with intuition, and remain steady in our realization that all men are Sons of God. We should not let the subconscious distortions or conditionings of another person involve us and cause us inconvenience. But, on the other hand, we do not have to pray for protection either. *In the World of Reality, isn't everything already complete and perfect? Doesn't right action always prevail? Then, why be double-minded and pray for protection from that which, in Truth, has no reality and no power?* "He that dwelleth in the secret place of most high, shall abide under the shadow of the Almighty!"

We do not need to pray for the overcoming of habits or tendencies of ourselves or others, in a specific manner; *we have but to realize a greater measure of God-consciousness* and this alone will adjust all matters properly.

It is quite easy to tell how spiritually aware we are. If we are still struggling with outer effects, if we are self-centered and ego-motivated, we have not yet arrived. If, on the other hand, we remain established in the realization of our God-nature, if we are selfless and have no sense of being apart from God, we are true initiates.

Absolute reliance upon the Infinite in all situations, moment by moment, is the way of the initiate. As a result of this inner reliance we find order and harmony is the law of our life. Desiring nothing of the outer world, we find that we possess it all. We live in eternity, observing the passing scenes. Outer conditions change constantly but we change not. We observe the processes of birth, change and death in the outer realms but we are not moved by appearances. Worlds are formed, evolve and fade away; souls lose their way and become hopelessly lost, only to awaken from the dream so completely that not a memory of it remains; the cycle of creation continues; but we are the same, established forever in God.